MAJC IN ENGINEERING

MAJORING IN ENGINEERING

How to Get from Your Freshman Year to Your First Job

JOHN GARCIA

THE NOONDAY PRESS
Farrar, Straus and Giroux
New York

Copyright © 1995 by John Garcia
All rights reserved
Published in Canada by HarperCollins*CanadaLtd*
Printed in the United States of America
First edition, 1995

LIBRARY OF CONGRESS CATALOGING-IN-PUBLICATION DATA
Garcia, John.
Majoring in engineering : how to get from your freshman year to
your first job / John Garcia.—1st ed.
p.   cm.
Includes bibliographical references.
1. Engineering—Vocational guidance.   I. Title.
TA157.G325   1995   620'.0023—dc20   95-6749   CIP

Excerpt from *The Scholarship Book* by Daniel J. Cassidy and Michael J. Alves
copyright © 1993 by Daniel J. Cassidy and Michael J. Alves,
reprinted by permission of Prentice Hall.

To my daughters, Juliana and Jaclyn—
May you inherit my love
of the engineering profession.

ACKNOWLEDGMENTS

When I was first approached about this project by an old high school friend of mine, Carol Carter, my initial reaction was: "I'm a scientist—an engineer—not a writer!" As I thought through my initial feelings, however, I realized there was an opportunity here. I was in the middle of documenting two large tasks at work. One required a significant amount of writing and the other a significant amount of editing. Both tasks demanded technical expertise and know-how, but I realized that my writing skills needed a tune-up. This project allowed me that opportunity, and I know that I've benefited both personally and professionally from it. Thanks, Carol, for thinking of me.

Numerous engineering friends and colleagues provided substance and credibility to this book. Their many hours of oral and written responses to my questionnaires were truly insightful. Without their encouragement, this book would not have been possible. My thanks to Dawn Cowan, Steve Doerr, Ingrid Eng, Rich Engstrom, Doug Gapp, Bill Garcia, Pauline Goolsby, Tommy Goolsby, Dave Kozlowski, Samantha Lapin, John Patterson, Dennis Roach, Jon Rogers, Gregg Skow, Keri Sobolik, Steve Sobolik, Steve Wilson, Stephanie Witkowski, Walt Witkowski, and Mary Young.

Many people contributed to the vision and mechanics of this book. My thanks to Elisabeth Kallick Dyssegaard, my editor, for giving me the opportunity to write it. Thanks also to Joan Mathieu for reviewing my manuscript in detail and making good comments and suggestions.

My heartfelt thanks to my wife, Gisele, who supported and encouraged me in completing this project, regardless of life's twists and turns. Without her, I wouldn't have done it!

CONTENTS

1 *Quantifying MY Engineering Qualities* 3

2 *Quantifying YOUR Engineering Qualities . . . Do You Want to Be an Engineer?* 8

3 *Do You Have What It Takes?* 22

4 *But What Kind of Engineering . . . ?* 31

5 *Which Engineering School to Choose* 52

6 *You've Finally Arrived at School* 77

7 *Working Part-Time* 90

8 *Being an Upperclassman* 102

9 *I Am an Engineer . . . Now What?* 112

10 *Consider an Advanced Degree . . . and Other Options* 126

Appendix: Associations and Organizations for the Engineering Student 133

MAJORING IN ENGINEERING

■ 1 ■

QUANTIFYING *MY* ENGINEERING QUALITIES

In the Beginning . . .

I knew at a very young age that I wanted to be an engineer. I can remember sitting in my room at the desk where I stored all of my tools and worldly secrets—pennies, paper clips, rubber bands, sticks, paper, glue, string, drawings, Play-Doh sculptures, Lincoln Log pieces—and *thinking, creating*, and losing track of time for many quiet hours. I showed my mom what I had made with my own hands, proud that I had created these items with the *resources* available to me.

But *logical, creative* thinking and a sense of accomplishment apply to many aspects of our lives. So what were the clues? How did I know I wanted to be an engineer?

I was fortunate to have a sister who liked to break things, which I *fixed* before my mom discovered them. I was a *problem solver*. Once, my sister broke my Fisher-Price dial-a-sound toy. I didn't want to tell on her, so I *assessed* the damage, *studied* the inner workings, and *repaired* the toy with the tools from my worldly-secrets desk.

It Wasn't a Revelation . . . It Was More Like an Experiment

You're probably thinking that children who think creatively and use available resources to fix things and solve problems don't necessarily have engineering tendencies. Well, you're right, because these are qualities that most of us develop to survive in this world.

However, childhood was one big scientific experiment for me. How many children performed experiments outside school hours and actually enjoyed it? I'm sure that this was the first clue that a technical career lay ahead. Three specific examples come to mind.

Save-the-Turtles Experiment

My sisters and I each had small water turtles as pets. They lived in a simple kidney-shaped pool of tap water, with no filtration system. Much to our dismay, we discovered that each turtle died within a few days for no apparent reason. After buying at least two sets of turtles, my mom said, "No more turtles." It was getting too expensive to replace them.

I was unhappy, not only because our turtles were dying but because I couldn't figure out why they were dying. So I convinced my mom to buy more turtles by promising to study the topic further. I told her that I would find a way to extend the turtles' life span.

Even though I was in Mrs. Williams's second-grade class, I asked Mr. Pelkan, a fourth- and fifth-grade science teacher, about my water turtle dilemma. He told me that I needed a *hypothesis* (a word that I could barely say) before I could design an *experiment* for *results* (increased life expectancy of my turtles).

I theorized that if I cut back on their feeding and changed their water daily, then their life expectancy would increase.

Indeed I performed the experiments with the new turtles, and their life expectancy increased from a few days to a few weeks. When I announced my results to Mr. Pelkan, he said, "That's wonderful. Now, explain to me *why* their life expectancy increased." I decided that I polluted the tap water by providing too much food which eventually decayed. The turtles also polluted their own environment by excreting normal waste products, which poisoned their source of life. If their water wasn't changed frequently, then the turtles died.

As a result of this experience, I learned about the scientific process and the steps involved: Hypothesize, Experiment, Generate Data, Assimilate Results, and Draw Conclusions. It was fun.

The Oatmeal Optimization Routine

The save-the-turtles experiment taught me about basic scientific processes, but as I moved into the fourth and fifth grades, I discovered the importance of optimization in scientific thinking.

I was a very independent child; each morning starting at age eight, I insisted on making my own breakfast, combing my hair, brushing my teeth, and dressing myself. I was never the type to sleep late, jump out of bed, and rush out the door half ready for school. I always planned ahead.

Part of my morning ritual involved making a bowl of old-fashioned oatmeal for breakfast. This required accurate measurements and precise timing for the desired consistency. I decided I could optimize preparation time by performing multiple tasks at once. My routine went like this: I came into the kitchen, still in my pajamas, and measured the correct amount of water, which was set on the stove until boiling (two minutes). During the boiling time, I dashed into the bathroom to clean my face, brush my teeth, and comb my hair. When I came back to the stove, the water was just starting to boil, at which time I stirred in the oats.

After turning the fire down to a simmer, I went back to my bedroom to select my clothes and dress for the day, which took five minutes. When I returned to the stove, I turned off the gas, covered the saucepan, and let the oatmeal sit for two minutes, which allowed me to quickly make my bed.

After I reentered the kitchen to pour a glass of milk and get utensils, I spooned the oatmeal from the saucepan into a bowl. I ate the oatmeal and drank the milk in five minutes, at which time I was ready for school. The total time from awaking to leaving for school was fourteen minutes.

As time went on, I was able to whittle my fourteen-minute routine down to twelve minutes, at which point I decided I had reached a limit on my efficiency. Any more time off the twelve minutes would mean that I had to skip an activity, such as combing my hair or brushing my teeth. That was unacceptable.

The Pinewood Derby Challenge

"O.K., John," you're saying now, "you should have been an efficiency expert with the oatmeal optimization routine nonsense. And not only that, you're weird." Perhaps I wasn't a normal child, but you'll discover that optimizing scientific experiments or engineering designs is very important in the engineering field. You'll see how, as a Cub Scout, I turned optimization into a design engineering challenge.

A particularly interesting event sponsored by the Scouts is appropriately named the Pinewood Derby. The boys who participated were given an identical rectangular block of pinewood and assorted attachments to make a race car for a regional competition. The boy who created the best design usually won.

I hand-whittled my rectangular block into a smooth, rounded aerodynamic shape to reduce wind drag as much as possible. I also distributed my fixed amount of counterbalancing weights to optimize speed while considering friction in the wheels. One year, as a result of my careful efforts, I took second place with my race car, which I developed completely on my own. It was a great way to experiment with my first engineering design.

That's Not "Casz"

As I moved into my middle school and in particular my high school years, my scientific aptitude was not the "in thing" among my peers. In the lingo of my late 1970s high school years, it wasn't "casz." ("Casz" literally meant "casual" but loosely translated to "cool.") Technical fields were for "nerds, geeks, dweebs, and coneheads."

Although I was subject to peer pressures, I had two inherent qualities that helped me through this tough stage: independence and leadership. Consequently, I took all of the math and science courses that my high school offered. I started with biology in my sophomore year and completed physics in my senior year. My math courses started with algebra as a middle school student and ended with calculus as a senior. I enjoyed all of these courses and did well in them.

You Were a Nerd

Although my wife is still convinced that I must have been a nerd during high school, I was actually a "well-rounded nerd" with many friends and outside activities. I wrestled for two years in high school, hiked, rappelled, and rock-climbed with a coed Explorer Scout group. I also went four-wheeling with my friends through the mountainous terrain in Tucson, Arizona.

I had girlfriends, listened to rock music, and worked odd jobs (yard boy, house boy, fix-it boy, Little League umpire, etc.). I also played the violin in the high school orchestra and took private piano lessons. All of these activities and experiences contributed to my well-being as a whole person who had engineering tendencies.

Transforming MY Qualities into YOUR Insights

Even though I had scientific aptitude at a young age, getting through engineering school was not easy. It was hard work. Throughout my college years, I had doubts and fears, and occasionally became disillusioned, like any college student. But I made it and earned a B.S. in civil engineering (1984) from the University of Arizona. I received my M.S. degree in civil engineering (1985) from Purdue University. I am currently manager of the Mechanical and Climatic Testing Department at Sandia National Laboratories in Albuquerque, New Mexico. I have a very challenging, satisfying, and rewarding career which I would not change for anything.

How YOU Can Do It

I've shared with you some of my earliest childhood experiences: thinking, creating, assessing, repairing, solving problems, performing scientific experiments, and designing race cars. Any one event may not be an indication of scientific aptitude, but the inclination toward the engineering field is certainly there.

What were your childhood experiences? Are there any indications of scientific aptitude? The stories that I've told so far represent just one in a wide array of potential clues. I seriously doubt that any other person has had the same experiences that I've had.

And so how do I extract your unique engineering qualities, define them for you, and move you in the engineering direction? I can't do that alone, but I know many engineers who may share your experiences. We can help you in selecting your technical field of interest.

When engineers approach problems, they initially set discrete "stepping-stones" (called sigma values) which lead to extremes from the norm. Eventually, they reach an extreme boundary, beyond which everything remains practically unchanged. Using this methodology, they place bounds on the problem, and study interesting points in between.

"But what does this sigma stuff have to do with MY engineering aptitude?" you ask yourself.

Well, it's like this. If I survey my colleagues, ask them the right questions, and generate good data, then I can tell you about their collective experiences, which allows me to assess the limits of their engineering aptitude and highlight discrete points in between. You will probably discover your aptitude lies somewhere between the extremes. If not, then you'll discover that you may not have the engineering aptitude.

Read this book before entering engineering school! Save yourself at least four years of misery if engineering is not right for you, because it's tough enough even if you have the aptitude. For those of you who discover your engineering aptitude, read this book again! You'll discover how others have made it through this process, leading you to a satisfying engineering career.

■ 2 ■

QUANTIFYING *YOUR* ENGINEERING QUALITIES . . .
Do You Want to Be an Engineer?

What's the Right Answer for You?

You've just read about some of my early engineering experiences. But looking back at the pieces of my puzzle won't reveal any clues about your engineering future. Or will it? Remember that my past is unique; yours is too. What is important about my story, however, is that I discovered my interests by using scientific methodology. My hypothesis proposed that my engineering mind surfaced at a young age. From there, I generated good data that traced my interest in the engineering field.

What is the right answer for you? Would you enjoy developing high explosives for a chemical research plant? Or designing fighter aircraft in the aerospace industry? Or would you find it a miserable grind to get through the daily task of performing an engineering job? Let's study the "Do you want to be an engineer?" question by using the scientific thought process. I will provide the framework from which you can assess your engineering qualities, tendencies, or talents (or lack thereof), and you can then draw your own conclusions. Hopefully, I can give you some good insights along the way.

The Garcia Childhood Experience Principle

Most scientists aspire to leave a mark on their expert field of study. In technical circles, a mark is defined as a significant advancement, improvement, or breakthrough which has been developed by an individual or group of individuals who promptly choose a unique name for their discovery. In chemistry, the discoverer of a new element on the periodic chart can choose whatever name he or she wants. When Glenn T. Seaborg discovered the element plutonium (Pu), he named it after the planet Pluto. Many scientists have numerical units named after them (Kelvin, Fahrenheit, Coulomb), while others have solution methods or laws named in their honor (Bernoulli, Mohr, Hook).

I am striving to leave my mark in engineering too. What I am proposing to you is the Garcia Childhood Experience Principle for Engineering. (At last, my very own theorem, although it sounds more like a new discovery in child psychology.) The principle states that childhood experiences hold the clues that, when revealed, could lead you to a satisfying engineering career or steer you clear of a miserable time.

As a budding young engineering protégé, you should be inquisitive and ask yourself, "How valid is the Garcia Childhood Experience Principle for Engineering? Should I participate in the process? Will the results be realistic?" The rigorous scientist would first question my notion that the principle is indeed a principle. Performing an experiment on myself (i.e., surveying my own childhood experiences) and drawing the conclusion that it related to my future engineering career is somewhat anecdotal; it relies on a gut feeling. In the technical community, an anecdotal finding is not a principle.

However, it is not my intention to develop a new principle. Rather, I have a good feeling that if you explore your childhood experiences for clues, then you might discover a latent engineering tendency that could get you thinking about a lifetime commitment. I think you should take the chance and participate in the process, while understanding that the results are not based on rigorous scientific principles. But that's O.K., because many engineering problems are not well understood anyhow. Oftentimes, engineers just rely on their best judgment in solving problems; you should just rely on your best judgment too.

Take Your Shoes Off, Lie Down, and Close Your Eyes . . .

In order to assess your engineering aptitude, I will ask you two simple questions, using the Garcia Childhood Experience Principle as a model. I have chosen to divide this process into two parts. The first section will explore your earliest childhood memories related to engineering. The second section will examine your more current experiences, which provide more obvious clues to your engineering aptitude. In both sections, I will suggest memory-jogging examples for you and discuss how today's engineers responded to my self-assessment plan.

SELF-ASSESSMENT SECTION I

Question 1. What early childhood memories suggest that you might like an engineering career? Summarize and explain below or on a separate sheet of paper.

Clue 1. Examine your family or close family friends.

Was your father, mother, or any other influential family member an engineer? As you probably know, childhood role models can have a lifelong impact on us. Parents are probably the most influential role models we have, although it is possible that an extended-family member, an aunt or uncle, could have influenced you as well.

Gregg Skow is a systems engineer who grew up in his father's engineering footsteps. He says, "My father was an electrical engineer by schooling and a mechanical engineer by trade. He used these skills around the house. He was always fixing or building something. I only acted as his gofer, but I always watched and learned from him." Pauline Goolsby had a similar situation, growing up with a dad who was a math teacher. She says, "He taught me that I must be capable of doing what boys do." As a result of his influence, Pauline became more determined than ever to complete her industrial engineering degree.

Clue 2. Examine your hobbies or interests as a child by thinking about the following.

What toys did you play with? Consider a memory of playing with Legos. Small projects like constructing airports, buildings, or chairs might be significant if you recall a fascination for this activity. Or perhaps you had an Erector Set, and you were intrigued by A-frame structures. Maybe creating Popsicle-stick houses was your favorite activity.

Dennis Roach, an aerospace engineer, was the ultimate toy enthusiast and game player as a young child. He remembers having the world's biggest collection of Tinkertoys, and he built a large carnival-like village complete with a Ferris wheel with moving parts. He and his sister also built Lincoln Log villages that were quite elaborate. He was resourceful with his building materials, and Popsicle-stick structures were not uncommon in many of his creations.

The games you played as a child may not have been so formal. Jon Rogers, a mechanical engineer, remembered playing number games. As the prices of fruits, vegetables, and canned goods were punched into the adding machine, he quickly added them up before the cashier hit the subtotal button. Jon says, "I was usually correct."

Did you like to fix things or figure out how they work? Did you wonder how objects fit together to form something useful? Maybe you recall fixing your tricycle or bicycle with simple tools, like a screwdriver, a pair of pliers, or an adjustable wrench. Perhaps you had a collection of models (airplanes, cars, battleships) that you assembled with a little guidance from an influential adult. If you enjoyed following assembly instructions and learning about individual components in a piece of hardware, then you may have discovered another useful clue.

Tommy Goolsby, a mechanical engineer, explained that he really enjoyed hands-on experiences as a child. He says, "I was fascinated with tools, and since my dad was in the home-building business, I had access to lots of them." Making plans and building things alongside his father had a significant impact on his decision to study mechanical engineering. Jon Rogers had a similar experience with his family's plumbing business. For as long as Jon could remember, afternoons, weekends, and summers were spent in the shop "helping" his dad work on projects. He says, "Mechanical devices always interested me."

Did you ever set up experiments? What were your favorite school activities? One logical clue is your participation in an elementary school science fair. Did you and your friends ever research the planets to understand gaseous makeup or movements for school science day? Did your Cub Scout group study crystal growth for a chemistry project? Perhaps you took your own initiative to experiment. Did you ever do any of the following?

- Put water outside on frigid nights to save energy and understand ice formation
- Have a moth collection (ant farm, toad farm, bug farm, etc.) and try to duplicate the natural environment as closely as possible in a jar
- Have a pet tarantula and study its creepy movements
- Have a rock collection that was categorized by type (color, size, shape)

Tommy Goolsby took advantage of many science fair opportunities. Tommy says, "When I entered middle school, I participated in a junior science seminar that held Saturday workshops. I remember experimenting with different kinds of propellant for rocket motors and various gunpowders." Mary Young, another mechanical engineer, participated in science fairs in other cities. She says, "I had science teachers who were really good with kids, and they encouraged me to participate in scientific activities."

What did you do for entertainment as a child? The answer to that question may not be earth-shattering, but there may be clues here too. Did you have an interest in the following reading materials?

- Science-fiction comic books
- "How things work" books
- *Twenty Thousand Leagues under the Sea*
- *Scientific Weekly Reader* (or some magazine similar to it)

What were your favorite movies or television programs? Did you admire James Bond's futuristic, high-technology gadgetry? Or were you a *Star Trek* fan who appreciated Scotty's insights into "warp factors" and the *Enterprise*'s capabilities?

Rich Engstrom, a nuclear engineer, says, "My childhood was dominated by reading and sports. I read everything I could get my hands on, from scientific novels through encyclopedias. It opened a whole world of possibilities for me, and I'm sure that this contributed an enormous amount to my understanding of the world and what it had to offer as I grew up." Jon Rogers was more specific about his reading activities as a child. He says, "When I was young, I read many of the Tom Swift books, which were very futuristic. We also had the Time-Life Natural Science library at home, and I read this for entertainment."

Clue 3. Not every engineer had technical interests as a child.

Samantha Lapin, a nuclear engineer, doesn't remember having the technical bug at an early age. She says, "I wish I could say that I knew from an early age that this was what I wanted to do, but that simply is the opposite of what is true. The only thing I remember *commenting* on at the age of ten was that I wanted to be a doctor. But I really find it tough to link this to my ultimately landing in engineering, since I have no idea why I ever said that. If I had had these formative experiences, I'm convinced that I would be on my way to my *second* Nobel Peace Prize and spending a lot less time on work-related reading in the evenings."

Scientific opportunities were not readily available to her as a child, she says. "The elementary school I attended did not have science experiments, fairs, or contests of any kind. Also, my parents are in the wholesale shoe business, so there were no scientific discussions taking place at my house."

Because Samantha's experiences don't fit the other engineers' stories, she shows that not all people fit the Garcia Childhood Experience Principle. Just because you may not have an engineering "revelation" in early childhood does not mean that you won't become an engineer. If you fall in this category, then read on!

SELF-ASSESSMENT SECTION II

If you discovered a few "engineering aptitude" clues in Self-Assessment Section I, then great! But many of these early childhood events could lead you anywhere—perhaps into marine biology or physics. So let's explore events in your teenage years for more specific and focused information.

Question 2. What current activities might lead you to an engineering career? Summarize and explain below or on a separate sheet of paper.

Clue 1. Are there influential people who have helped you sort out your interests? Are you receiving guidance or direction from figures of authority?

Mentors

Interactions with adults at this critical age are very important—even crucial—for the person that we eventually become. Your family members (parents, grandparents, older siblings, etc.) continue to mold and shape your thinking, and it is imperative that you take their experiences into account now.

Figures of authority outside the family might have significant influence on you as well. Consider the geometry teacher who explained proofs to you until you understood them. How about the physics teacher who signed you up for your first science fair project? Was there an interested school counselor who spent a few extra moments guiding your future? As you consider any of these influential people, does the concept of a *mentor* come to mind?

You may have had a mentor or several mentors throughout your teenage years and not realized it. A mentor is one whom you trust and respect—a person whose opinion you value greatly. His or her advice, knowledge, or insight is often very valuable. Mentors can be anyone from your mother's best friend to the family clergyman. It certainly does not have to be anyone in a technical field.

If you've discovered that you have or have had a mentor, by all means keep in touch with that person. Review with him or her your personality traits. Do you both agree that you have what it takes?

Other engineers discussed their mentor stories with me. See if you can relate to them.

Gregg Skow remembered his father's influence on him:

> My teenage years were spent helping my father with hands-on work around the house and in the garage. I enjoyed those times and I learned a lot about the commonsense side to engineering. For example, if Dad and I were building a table out of wood, and we miscalculated one of the dimensions, we often discovered the mistake before cutting it incorrectly. This was because we looked at the piece of wood we were about to cut, and we could just tell that this would not work with the desired end product. So I learned from Dad that scoping out the problem and predicting the desired results before any activity took place was a time- and cost-saving activity. This process is important in the engineering field.

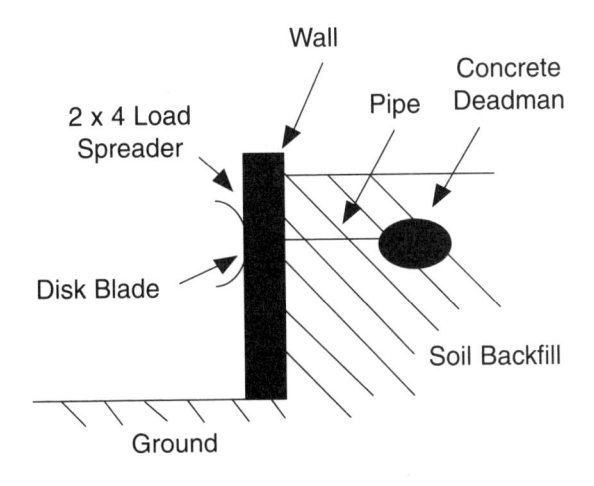

Figure 2-1. One of Jon Rogers's early design efforts

Jon Rogers's engineering experiences became more explicit as he entered his teenage years too.

> My parents' cabin in Minnesota was our summer home. There was always plenty of work to do on it. One summer, we had to replace a retaining wall. With Dad supervising, my older brother and I had to figure out how to re-lay a block wall and keep it from falling over. (The wall had approximately six feet of soil backfill.) For support we set some deadmen in concrete with disk blades on pipes which penetrated the wall. (See Figure 2-1.) Participating in projects like this with Dad doing "seat of the pants" design established a curiosity in me. I wanted to understand how engineering design adequacy was determined, and I thought that there must be a better way than trial and error.

Although most engineers had experiences with family members, some had experiences with school officials. Dennis Roach recalls a conversation with his guidance counselor (a priest) at his Catholic high school in Niagara Falls, New York. He says, "I went to ask him about engineering career information, and I remember being interested in the aerospace engineering curriculum. He was able to satisfy my curiosity."

Clue 2. What subjects have you studied the most? In what areas do you excel?

Coursework

I'm going to list typical subjects which you may be studying now or in the future. Can you relate to any of these hypothetical experiences?

1. Math

- Algebra. I enjoyed solving algebraic equations, and I can still recite the quadratic equation from memory, but I had a tough time with some of the story problems.
- Geometry. The Pythagorean theorem was intriguing, but I couldn't handle those proofs. My teacher was nice, and I could relate to him because he helped out with the wrestling team.
- Trigonometry. The relationships between sine, cosine, and tangent functions were easy to apply to real-world problems. My teacher made this topic fun and interesting.
- Analytical Geometry. I remember getting all of the right answers on my homework and exams. I liked helping other people understand some of the mathematical concepts.
- Calculus. The slope of lines (first derivatives) and areas under curves (integrals) had real-world applications. My teacher reviewed each new concept (slowly) in a logical manner that was easy to follow.

2. Sciences

- Earth and Physical Sciences. These classes were a great way to start a series of scientific courses yet to come.
- Biology. The study of single-cell creatures was fascinating. I remember the paramecia cell division experiment quite well.
- Chemistry. The laboratory experiments were my favorite portion of this class because we created great mixtures of basic elements, which liberated large amounts of energy. I was able to quantify these exothermic reactions.
- Physics. The study of object movements (kinematics) piqued my curiosity about gravity. I remember my teacher's explanation about the constant acceleration that all objects experience on earth.
- Computer Sciences. I was interested in computer hardware, so I assembled my own computer from parts such as a motherboard, hard-disk drive, power supply, etc. I also wrote basic programs in my computer class.

3. Industrial Arts

- Computer-Aided Drafting (CAD). I sketched race car designs on the CAD system at school. I learned how to read engineering drawings as a result of this course.
- Machine Shop. I designed and built the metal framework for my go-cart as a class project. Many of the small metal pieces were generated using a lathe.
- Wood Shop. I designed and crafted a small table and a set of chairs for my little sister.
- Automotive Shop. I learned the intricate workings of an internal-combustion engine. The hands-on experience of working on staff cars was invaluable to understanding the mechanical design of an automobile.
- Electrical Shop. I started the course building a doorbell and ended the course wiring an entire house. I understood a lot about electricity as a result.

When I asked my colleagues about their favorite subjects, they responded with a common theme—science and math. Does that surprise you? It shouldn't. Nearly all of them took all of the science (earth or physical science, biology, chemistry, and physics) and math (typically algebra, geometry, trigonometry, analytical geometry, and calculus) courses available to them. However, my colleagues were *well rounded* in their curriculum and interests. They mentioned the following courses too.

- Shop Classes (welding, woodworking, automotive, etc.)
- Mechanical Design Courses
- Architectural Design Courses
- Basic Art Classes
- Literature
- History

Clue 3. What extracurricular activities interest you? What clubs are you associated with?

Obviously, there's more to life than just coursework. I'd like you to think about extracurricular school activities as well. I realize that there are many activities available to students, but concentrate on the intellectual clubs rather than the sporting or social clubs. Again, I'll propose a few examples that you might relate to.

- Chess Club. I joined the chess club because I enjoyed strategic, critical, logical thinking. I participated in district-wide tournaments with other schools.
- Debate Team. I prepared for all of my debates by studying the issues using sound reasoning and logic. I always highlighted my opponent's oversimplified, unprepared position, which gave me the competitive edge during the debates.
- Math Club. We challenged one another to solve brainteasers in the shortest amount of time.
- Science Club. The field trips helped me understand the scientific world. In particular, I remember visiting the observatory and gazing at the stars. The astronomer told us how to perform simple calculations concerning orbital motion.

Clue 4. What are your hobbies and interests outside of school activities?

The interests that develop during your high school years will probably stay with you for a lifetime. Natural tendencies, habits, or traits that define you as a unique person may be very evident during these years. Capabilities and interests in a technical field may be determined by examining your hobbies—activities that no other person is forcing or persuading you to do. See if you can relate to any of these hypothetical activities.

- Gun Club. I was an active member of the gun club with my family. We loaded our own shells with explosives and went out once a month for skeet-shooting practice. I remember my dad requiring me to completely disassemble a gun and clean it using safe gun-handling techniques. I studied the ballistic handbooks to determine optimum loading densities and ballistic trajectory information. It was important to understand basic gun technology because an overload of explosives in a shell could cause excess pressure in the gun breech, which is extremely dangerous.
- Motorcycle/Motocross/Go-Cart Racing. I always disassembled my go-cart to modify existing off-the-shelf technology to make it better. I found that I could optimize my engine performance, which allowed me to reduce mechanical problems. I rebuilt my own cart after each race.
- Home Build-It Projects. My parents were home-project fiends. They were always tearing something in the house apart and putting it back together. I had a tendency to follow right along with them. Whether it was installing a new bathroom or adding a garage, I was involved

in the planning, designing, and building of our latest home feature. I enjoyed working with plans and tools.
- Home Fix-It Projects. Whenever we weren't tearing apart the kitchen or modifying the back bedroom, we were keeping the house in good repair. I learned that almost every mechanical item tends to break if you ignore routine maintenance long enough. One time, I helped to figure out why the washing machine broke. (Can we salvage the transmission on the washer?) And another time, I discovered why the hot-water heater wasn't working. (If it's electric, maybe one of the heating elements went out.) We fixed almost everything ourselves, which saved us money.
- Scouting Activities. I was involved in Scouting activities that exposed me to engineering-related projects. I remember many environmental concerns that formed the basis for some of our merit badge completion activities. Some of the titles of these projects were:

—"Clean Up the Air Quality Project"
—"How to Prevent Ground Water Contamination Project"
—"The Wildlife Water Retention Project"

We also went on many Saturday hikes collecting rocks in the mountains. We had a guest geological speaker who accompanied us one morning. She pointed out basic features such as anticlines, synclines, and faults. I never thought to study geological features until she pointed them out.

If you can't relate to any of the above examples, you should definitely get involved in some of these scientific activities. Below I've listed a few more examples from other engineers.

Steve Doerr, an aerospace engineer, had an interest in model airplanes. He says, "I was interested in jets because my dad was in the Air Force. I started flying model airplanes as a hobby in high school, and even after nine or ten years of college and graduate school, I still find the study of turbulence and shock-wave interactions interesting. There are still a lot of unknowns in aerospace engineering and no canned solutions. I enjoy the challenge."

Another common hobby mentioned by engineers was fixing cars. John Patterson, a civil engineer, says, "I always fixed my car since my dad always fixed his own; it saved us money. But by far the thing I enjoyed most about fixing cars was stereo installation. I installed and upgraded car stereos and speakers for myself and all of my friends."

During his teenage years, Dennis Roach shared a hobby with his neighbors across the street in Lewiston, New York. He says, "The neighbors had every kind of tool imaginable and lots of scrap materials. I remember building go-carts from scraps of wood, as well as a motorized minibike from an old lawn-mower engine. It was a great hands-on experience."

Clue 5. What are your work experiences?

As most teenagers begin to develop their sense of independence, they have a need to earn their own money and contribute to their own well-being. That means finding a job that pays for gas, movies, or other entertainment activities. Besides the usual newspaper delivery or busboy job, do you have any work experiences directly related to engineering?

Some high schools offer a career exploration opportunity, such as an internship program. Did you volunteer your time to work for class credit? Perhaps you're working part-time for a few bucks as an office gofer, clerk, or secretary in a materials engineering firm. Or maybe you're working for a large defense contractor firm that has an organized program for work-study students.

There are summer jobs as well. Perhaps you would like to have the unique experience that John Patterson had in his teenage years.

> My parents were divorced, so I spent many of my summers with my father, who is a civil engineer too. I worked with him in places such as Seattle building four-story prefabricated housing units that were then shipped to Alaska's North Slope. I also worked with him constructing a smelter in the central mountains of Iran. As a result of these work experiences, I learned that being a civil engineer in construction meant building a variety of different and interesting things.

Jot Down Your Thoughts

If you haven't already done so, answer the questions in Self-Assessment Sections I and II, keeping the clues and experiences of other engineers in mind. You can use the space provided in this book or you can write more detailed information on another sheet of paper.

Compare your responses to the examples. Where do you stand now? Are you more comfortable with your potential engineering tendencies than you were before you responded? Did you discover anything about yourself in the process? Better yet, did you discover your engineering aptitude? If the answer is a resounding "Yes," then great. That's the purpose of this chapter. But if your answer is "I don't know" or simply "No," then read on. I am going to present another viewpoint on these experiences that might help you.

If you were left cold by this discussion of engineering aptitude, and you don't have any experiences to relate to, then consider the thoughts of Samantha Lapin. Looking back on her childhood, she couldn't think of any experiences that had anything to do with her nuclear engineering career. And so she wanted to pass along the following information.

> Ninth grade is where I really got *off* track (never mind that I was never really on it). My attention turned away from math and most academics of any kind toward friends, tennis, and art. You see, I had an excellent role model in *art*; my grandfather is a nationally recognized photographer and artist. So I explored my potential talents in this area, and I participated in art shows, contests, and tutoring sessions. If you really want to know just how *far away* I was from engineering, I still remember today telling my friends that I really did not care how the lights came on (or how anything else worked, for that matter) as long as they did. Youch! Sign her up for engineering classes!

And so there you have it. Samantha is my reality check on the Garcia Childhood Experience Principle hypothesis. Although it appears that the majority of practicing engineers had similar childhood experiences that led them down the engineering path, not everyone falls into these neat bins. If you find that you can relate better to Samantha, all is not lost in the discovery of your engineering aptitude. We still haven't covered your experiences in the near future. Read on!

· 3 ·

DO YOU HAVE WHAT IT TAKES?

It's Not by Osmosis

The engineering aptitude test in Chapter 2 was perhaps a nice verification exercise for some and an enlightening process for others. You may have known, just as I knew very early, that engineering was your destiny; and it was comforting for you to verify this. Or you may be still unsure of your particular interests—that's O.K. too. Regardless, you must realize that your engineering aptitude is important only if it develops into something useful.

You're probably wondering why it is important to develop your engineering tendencies. Aren't straight A's in math and science courses good enough? Well, take it from my personal experience, a good engineer is composed of a lot more than superior math and science scores. Although grades can be an indication of strengths and weaknesses, they're not everything.

Consider the high school student who was very bright and performed quite well in school, especially in math and science courses. The student rarely studied, and was busy with lots of nonacademic activities—primarily daydreaming. The student was lucky that his natural intellect let him get by with the least amount of effort possible. I know I was a little like that as a teenager. We've all crossed paths with this type of student, or been there ourselves.

Consider Gregg Skow's summary of his high school study habits and grades: "I didn't need to study to get good grades. I didn't know at the time that something was lacking in my overall education, but now I know better." Initially, Gregg wasn't thinking *logically* about his coursework. The "getting by" with good grades because he was intelligent was not the best way to go through school. He realized after entering college that he needed to understand concepts as well. If he had worked harder in high school, his transition to engineering school would have been easier.

So let's spend time assessing the necessary traits to get you through engineering school. The two most important qualities for your engineering success are *logical* thinking and *discipline*. If you keep these concepts in mind, it may be easier for you to achieve the engineering career that you've been dreaming about.

Plan, Plan, Plan

The first step in logical thinking is to develop a plan. It's an important part of any engineering project, because it will force you to think about how you will accomplish your task. If you can't develop a plan to complete a project, then you probably won't complete it. Similarly, if you don't develop a plan to complete your engineering degree, then you may not complete it.

When I was a young college student, I could have used a better *plan of attack*—used a little more logic to take more control of my destiny. Many of my potential career paths were selected arbitrarily without much forethought. Certainly, this is not a good engineering approach to solving a problem. So what can you learn from my experience on the subject of planning? Well, as my father used to tell me: "Learn from *other* people's mistakes, so that you don't fall into the same traps and waste a lot of *your* time!" Take control over your future. Guarantee your success by establishing a plan to complete your engineering degree.

Planning Your Engineering Field of Study

Choosing to study civil engineering as opposed to many other potential engineering fields was purely happenstance on my part. There wasn't a shred of forethought. I've already told you that I knew at a young age that I wanted to be an engineer, but what kind? I really didn't know that engineering work could vary so widely: designing mechanical parts, analyzing stress concentrations, developing wastewater treatment processes, directing excavation or tunneling projects, engineering chemical reactions, designing computer and electronic hardware . . . and the list goes on.

Fortunately for me, my father had a friend who was a civil engineer and owned his own company. My father asked his friend if I might tag along while he worked. As it turned out, I only worked with this man one Saturday when I was in high school (pro bono, of course). The task that I was assigned had something to do with holding a surveying rod for a man who ran a transit, while the civil engineer recorded elevation readings. The project dealt with surveying a series of lots for a development of private residences. Once the day's work was completed, the civil engineer placed his professional engineering (PE) stamp of approval on the drawings. (A PE stamp means that a licensed engineer assumes responsibility and liability for his work.) It seemed neat to me that he had this PE stamp; it was a mark of distinction and power in my eyes.

Because of that small experience, I later decided to study civil engineering at the University of Arizona, where I learned, by sheer luck, that I liked it. Not much of a plan; not much logical thinking.

Chapter 4 will discuss different types of engineering professions, so that you can make informed decisions about your engineering education. It will help you develop the first part of your plan.

Selecting a School

How did I know that the University of Arizona was the school that suited my civil engineering interests? I didn't. I remember wanting to go to the University of Colorado at Boulder for other reasons; I wanted to ski in the Rocky Mountains. Did the University of Colorado at Boulder even have a civil engineering program? I still don't know to this day, but choosing a school to meet my engineering needs didn't even cross my mind.

A little bit of informed planning could have put me at other schools. I had no idea what the civil engineering school curriculum was like, what the professors were like, what the ratio of student to teachers was, how well the school was funded, what the nationwide ranking of the civil engineering department was . . . and on and on. I could have done a little more research into the various schools and been much more informed. As it turned out, the civil engineering department at the University of Arizona was pretty good.

Chapter 5 will help you decide, logically, which engineering school you should attend.

Finding a Job in an Engineering Career

When I graduated with my bachelor's degree, I wanted to forge ahead into the workforce, because I was determined to make a significant contribution to our society as an engineer—I was somewhat idealistic.

As a result, I did a fair amount of *planning* looking for my first job as an engineer. My main source of information was the career placement center at the University of Arizona, and I spent many hours investigating the job opportunities it promoted. Each week, beginning in my first semester as a senior in college, I pored throuth the card catalogues and job announcements, looking for that high-paying civil engineering job that I always dreamed of.

There were many opportunities available at the time I graduated in 1984. Many of the mining firms were hiring, several of the small consulting firms were interviewing, and lots of defense contractors were hungry for young engineers. With each job opportunity, I carefully researched the company, got a general idea of its past, current, and future work. I knew that if I did some research up front, then I could better decide if I wanted to interview with the company. Also, if I chose to interview with the company, then it was a great way to prepare.

I remember trying to memorize facts and figures about particular companies; I wanted to be well informed and interested in the interviews. Maybe they might want me to spout off company statistics or understand the workings of their management system. What about salary, benefits, and vacation? Would I be expected to have prior knowledge of these issues? I really tried to absorb as much information as possible, so that the interviewer would be impressed with my knowledge of the company.

After all of this planning, researching, and preparing for job interviews, I received an unexpected phone call from a recruiter at Sandia National Laboratories. He had searched a card file at the University of Arizona career placement office, and he pulled my name because I had a high GPA in structural engineering. That's how I got an interview, and that's how I got a job.

Chapter 9 will detail a logical process to find your first job. Hopefully, your experiences won't come about by happenstance.

Your Planning Insights

Random events are a part of everyday living. It's highly unlikely that you've ever made it through an entire day without something slightly unexpected happening. However, there's a difference between planning every *hour* of your life, which you may have little control over, and planning your career destiny over a period of *years*, which you do have control over. Since the time scales are vastly different, the unplanned events usually affect your hourly schedule, but not your yearly plan. Transient activities will be overcome by large time periods!

So develop a long-term goal for yourself (choosing to be an engineer) and draft a plan to accomplish your long-term objective. Start by putting your goal on paper. After you've written your goal, divide your plan into manageable pieces. Consider a series of logical steps in this process:

- Plan your field of study; research it and understand it as best you can. (Chapter 4)
- Pick a group of potential engineering schools to attend. Do a background check on the engineering programs at each school. Start with some basic demographic information such as student population, school size and funding outlook, and student-to-teacher ratios. (Chapter 5)
- Work in your engineering field of interest while you're in school. Start gathering information on the opportunities available to you. (Chapter 9)

Don't feel compelled, just yet, to put pencil to paper answering the above questions. Each *planning* question is pretty intense and somewhat complex. I'll guide you through each topic. You'll have plenty of room to write your goals and plans throughout the rest of the book.

Stick with the Plan

If you think logically and develop a plan, but you don't follow it, then you'll never complete your engineering degree. In order to stick to your plan, you must develop a disciplined approach to your engineering education, because the curriculum is hard.

Consider Mary Young's situation. Mary says, "I didn't pursue engineering directly out of high school because women were actively discouraged from it at that time. Also, I thought it was an impossibly hard curriculum." Mary was a social worker and then a machinist before she became a mechanical engineer with a master's degree from the University of Arkansas. She was determined throughout her career to find an interest that suited her even though it took her some time to figure it out. Perhaps a good plan could have steered her in the right direction early on, saving her some time. No doubt, her stick-to-it attitude helped her reach her goal.

So how do you put your plan into action? Stick with it. It's not going to come easy—nothing ever does that's worthwhile. It's going to take some forethought, some time, some energy, and some natural talent. But without a disciplined approach to your engineering education, you won't succeed.

If you're still unsure of your natural talents or interest in engineering, try it for a while. At least take a few courses in engineering, along with other coursework. Give it your best shot, and if it doesn't work out, then that's O.K. Maybe you'll end up in the field at some later time in your life, just as Mary Young did. You'll have given it an honest chance.

Disciplined and Enthusiastic

Although you should methodically stick to your plan, be enthusiastic about it; otherwise you'll struggle with it. Be excited about exploring new things in a totally foreign field and about developing different talents or skills. Look forward to solving problems with a sense of accomplishment. But don't be reckless in your approach. I have a very good engineering friend who advised me that it's O.K. to keep dreaming, but keep your feet on the ground. She told me to keep my sights high, as high as I possibly could, but keep my sense of reality too. Remember, engineers are pragmatic people by nature, and we are typically tasked with providing real-world answers.

Disciplined with a Cause

Have you ever been dedicated to something that you truly believed in? Think about a marriage, a formal business contract, or a lifetime friendship. In all of these cases, one must commit to a person or activity that requires constant attention, care, evaluation, and change. The success of a marriage, friendship, or contract depends on the strength of your commitment. In a similar vein, you must approach your engineering education and career with equal dedication.

Commit yourself to the engineering field. Ask yourself a fundamental question. Do you believe in what you're doing? Ingrid Eng, a civil engineer with a consulting firm in New York City, says that "engineering is a challenging and stimulating profession, and I always remember that I am contributing to a better society." Although most professions provide a chance to better society in some way, Ingrid feels that her basic belief in what she is doing gives her a strong withsense of commitment to her work. It was the right thing to do with her life while helping to meet some of society's basic needs, such as infrastructure (designing roadways, bridges, buildings, etc.). Perhaps you can develop such an attitude in your engineering studies.

Disciplined Yet Flexible

Even the best-laid plans go awry. Don't worry. You'll make plenty of mistakes along your engineering education path. Your mistake might be as simple as a bad final exam grade, because you didn't study. Or it might be more serious, such as the realization that you've chosen the wrong field of engineering study. Relax! Whatever your dilemma is, remember that many practicing engineers have confronted the same issues and concerns, and have emerged unscathed by the experiences.

Consider Gregg Skow's college experiences:

> I started college in the field of mechanical engineering. I picked mechanical engineering simply because I had to choose one, and my brother went through the mechanical engineering college and seemed to enjoy it. But after a couple of years, I became disinterested. I thought that maybe engineering was not the right subject for me. So I transferred to business college. I took courses toward an accounting degree for one semester. I remember that I was able to work more hours on my night job and still maintain the same level of grades, but the challenge wasn't there and neither was the satisfaction.
>
> I discussed my dilemma with my father. I told him that I was pretty sure that I wanted to go back to the engineering college, but I didn't know which engineering field to study. He told me that the easiest engineering field to find jobs in was systems engineering (circa 1983). Knowing that not all graduates have an easy time finding jobs, I decided that picking a field with a large number of job opportunities was a good idea. I went to the systems engineering college for information on their curriculum, and subsequently enrolled in the college. Two and a half years later, I graduated.

Gregg had some major issues to cope with in the middle of his engineering education. After realizing his mistake (choosing mechanical engineering) and making some changes to his plan (moving out of and back into engineering studies), he turned his experiences into something *positive*. It isn't enough to accept an error without correcting the problem and learning from it. It might take you a few extra semesters to figure things out, but that's O.K. Don't give up!

Speaking of exploring other curricula, remember my friend Samantha Lapin, who gave me my reality check on childhood experiences? She has more insight into making corrections in college studies.

I entered college (circa 1980) all set to be an art major, when I went through a revelation that went something like this: "I am getting to be an art major leading to a career in an area where I really have no talent (Grandpa had it *all*) and I couldn't see myself spending eight hours a day drawing.

So there I was my freshman year looking for a major. I drummed up a weak recollection from fifth grade about wanting to be a physician (for no apparent reason), and I started taking pre-med classes. This went fine until biology and organic chemistry classes began and I really decided that this stuff was awful. So I turned to a good friend of mine who seemed very happy and was doing quite well in electrical engineering (one Diana King) and said, "Aaargh, what should I do with the rest of my life?" She suggested I look into engineering.

I had just finished reading a book on energy sources and Diana and I talked about it. She told me that there was a newly created discipline called energy engineering. So off I went to enroll in energy engineering classes. Once there for about a semester, I decided that I was particularly interested in nuclear energy since discussions of the atoms in previous classes (e.g., chemistry and physics) were always the most intriguing to me. As you may guess, I moved into nuclear engineering, where I found true bliss and happiness (together with true agony and unhappiness from studying *all* the time) and lived happily ever after . . . until graduate school.

Although Samantha readily admits she didn't have a plan of attack (none of us did), she made several changes of direction in her college studies. Discovering art, pre-med, and engineering is a lot of territory to cover in such a short period of time. Nonetheless, Samantha was not afraid to explore other avenues and make appropriate changes until she found something that suited her interests.

The End of the Pep Talk

As you may have realized by now, I've spent the last few pages trying to get you psyched for what's to come. However, there is a certain element of truth to Samantha's comment about engineering studies and "true agony and unhappiness from studying *all* the time," and I want to alleviate as much pain as possible for you. If you keep a few ideas and tools at your fingertips, life will be a whole lot easier as you enter the depths of engineering studies. Remember the following key concepts:

- **Set a goal.** Say, "I want to be an engineer!"
- **Develop a plan—logically.** Write down the steps needed to achieve your goal. (Remember, you'll have plenty of insight and suggestions for developing your plan throughout the rest of this book.)
- **Develop discipline.** Stick with the program; give it your best shot.
  —**Be enthusiastic** about exploring new things in a totally foreign field.
  —**Be committed** to the engineering field.
  —**Be flexible** by exploring new avenues, making changes, and learning from your mistakes.

▪ 4 ▪

BUT WHAT KIND OF ENGINEERING . . . ?

"Math and science were easy, but I didn't know which engineering field to choose," said Ingrid Eng. When she was a sophomore in high school, her father suggested that she should research the engineering field. Coincidentally, she recalls, she had a research paper due on careers in her English class, and she proceeded to drum up information on civil engineering. She learned that civil engineers work in both the office and the field and that they travel frequently. "This was very attractive to me, because I wanted a hands-on engineering field of study. Not only that, but traveling sounded like fun, especially to a young woman in high school!"

Many aspiring engineers go off to college with ill-defined engineering fields of study. Notions of working in the office and the field are quite vague; civil engineers are involved in many technical activities on a daily basis that an aspiring engineer should know about.

As you probably know by now, I strongly advocate good planning and research before entering a field of study. The first part of this process, choosing your discipline, involves a discussion of specific engineering fields so that you can get an overview of the profession. The second part outlines the modes within each discipline: theory (research and development), design, analysis, and testing. (After choosing an engineering discipline, do you want to research it, design it, analyze it, or test it?) Also, I'll review other career paths for engineers after they've worked a while: management, production and sales, or consulting. You'll be naturally drawn to some disciplines rather than others, and you'll have a general feel for the engineering profession.

What's an Engineer?

Before we get into the details of specific disciplines, I thought it might be best to define, succinctly, what an engineer is. Here's my definition:

"An engineer is a problem solver who uses technical means to make theory a reality."

The engineer assesses society's needs, formulates a problem, and solves the issue using theoretical tools based primarily on mathematics and scientific observations. Society's needs range from basic infrastructure issues (transportation networks, communications, water flow) to more exotic technologies (space travel, artificial-limb design, robotics). In the eyes of an engineer, all of these issues and technologies represent problems that need to be worked on or solved. On the basis of mathematical techniques and scientific observations, the engineer moves toward a usable solution—one that is practical and economically feasible. The resulting product, usually a piece of hardware or a working system, must function not only in its intended mode but in its predicted (futuristic) modes as well.

This definition is not unique to the engineering profession. Consider medicine. The physician solves your health concerns by making medical theory a reality. The reality is a cure for whatever ails you. Unfortunately, the medical profession doesn't have a cure for all of life's physical ailments. Similarly, the engineering profession doesn't have exact solutions for all engineering problems. However, we do have approximate solutions for problems, and in many situations that's O.K.

But don't head off to engineering school armed only with this broad definition of the profession. There are many specific engineering fields, each vastly different, that you need to consider. Let's examine the breadth of the different engineering fields first before we get to the specifics.

The Big Engineering Picture

Some engineering professions date back centuries, as old as Moses himself! All ancient societies built things (structures), needed water for crops (water flow or hydraulics), and moved (transportation). These activities or societal needs would fall in the civil engineering category. Explosive devices, like a bullet, and delivery mechanisms, like a black-powder gun, were engineered by early chemical or mechanical designers. However, the mechanical and chemical engineering disciplines, as well as mining engineering, were more the product of the 1800s industrial revolution than anything else. Society developed a technological need to support its ever changing world. Electricity ran machines in factories; explosives created holes through mountains for railroad movements. Engineering synergism developed during this time period.

Table 4-1 introduces a few of these "older," more traditional disciplines, with a list of specialties under each engineering field.

As society advanced into the twentieth century, so did the engineering professions: civil engineers design high-speed roadways and optimum transportation networks; mechanical engineers study space dynamics; chemical engineers study advanced synthetic materials such as artificial muscles; mining engineers develop safer underground blast techniques; electrical engineers study satellite communications. Not only have the traditional disciplines evolved over time but many new engineering fields have recently developed. Some of the new kids on the block include nuclear engineering, aerospace engineering, metallurgical engineering, systems and industrial engineering, and computer engineering. Another category, engineering mathematics, doesn't fit well into the traditional or newer disciplines, but it should be recognized as an engineering field. I'll also mention more specialized fields that are usually graduate-level study areas.

Civil Engineering

As I've mentioned before, civil engineering (CE) is perhaps one of the oldest engineering specialties. (I saw a T-shirt at a CE conference that said "Civil Engineering, the Second Oldest Profession!") The CE studies, designs, and analyzes basic engineering needs for society. Most of society's infrastructure is developed by the CE: roads, bridges, waterways, dams, sewage treatment systems, transportation networks, and other basic structures. Major CE study areas include:

1. *Structural.* Although I'll try to remain unbiased in my summaries of each study area, you must realize that this was my main field of study in school for both my bachelor's and my master's degree. I studied basic structural elements, such as beams, columns, plates, shells, and spheres, that were made from materials such as steel and reinforced concrete. What's so interesting about structural elements and their materials? Well, when they are loaded with static forces (i.e., forces that don't vary with time), I could predict how these elements would displace and I could determine corresponding stress values. The results of such analysis allowed me to design things such as multistory buildings, bridges, storage tanks, and concrete canoes. (Yes, I said concrete canoes; I'll have more to say about this design project later in the book.) For the first time in my life, I really felt that I was doing something useful with my natural tendencies toward math and science!

As I moved into graduate school, I studied structural dynamics, or the response of structural members to time-dependent forces. I was

Table 4-1. Traditional Engineering Disciplines

Civil	Mechanical	Chemical	Electrical	Mining
• Structural	• Power Generation	• Energy Resources	• Circuits	• Tunnel & Pit Design
• Wastewater	• Power Transmission	• Industrial Production	• Electromagnetics	• Rock Mechanics
• Hydraulic	• Power Application	• Environment & Waste Management	• Power Systems	• Safety
• Geotechnical		• Electronic Applications	• Control Systems	• Separation Techniques
• Transportation		• Bio-Products	• Signal Processing	
			• Computer	

trained to predict the structural response of a bridge or a multistory building if it was acted upon by a periodic force, such as a sinusoidal motion. Such methodologies are used in the design of earthquake-resistant structures. When the earth moves and causes a building to sway, take comfort in the fact that a structural dynamicist has predicted the movement of the structure and enabled it to respond without collapsing!

2. *Wastewater.* O.K., this doesn't sound like the most exotic field of study that one can imagine, but how exciting are bridge movements? Some people probably think it's like watching grass grow! Needless to say, wastewater engineers study ways to change contaminated sewage effluent into useful by-products. All modern cities have some kind of wastewater flow and collection system that must be properly engineered and designed. Through a series of baffled tanks, aerated ponds, and separation points, the effluent is changed into something useful such as water for irrigation systems. This process is critical to the functioning of society as we know it!

3. *Hydraulic.* The study of fluid flow as it applies to waterways, channels, canals, or other drainage methods allows the engineer to deal with water-flow problems. In high-density areas with lots of pavement and buildings, where does the water go after a heavy rainstorm? Unlike soil and other earthen materials, asphalt and concrete cannot absorb large quantities of water. Hopefully, the hydraulic engineer has done his quantity-flow calculations, directing the water into a network of capable culverts and channels that eventually lead to a riverbed or stream.

4. *Geotechnical.* Have you ever heard of a structure that settled over time? I know someone who built a house on soil that expanded and contracted with the slightest change in moisture content, which caused serious cracks in the house's foundation. These soil issues are the responsibility of a geotechnical engineer, who studies the foundations of structures and other "earthy" topics. The geotechnical engineer determines the in situ soil characteristics (water content, density, shear strength, etc.) of potential building sites and prepares a plan to provide adequate support. How do you think New York City's Manhattan Island supports so many large structures in such a small area? Some very competent rock formations provide a basis for a good foundation.

5. *Transportation.* How many horse-and-buggy routes had stoplights at intersections? This field of study is relatively new to the civil engineering profession. How many times have you cursed at a red light that seemed too long, and stopped you every time you approached the intersection? But you probably haven't cursed too many times if

the traffic engineer has studied his traffic-flow patterns correctly. The discipline might be best described as a study of logistics applied to roadways and vehicles. The transportation engineer might analyze traffic-flow patterns and design optimum traffic-light timing for a given network. He is responsible for designing bends and turns in roadways, providing safe sight distances, or determining safe vehicle maneuvering speeds. The engineer even studies types of roadway materials and how to improve their wear-and-tear characteristics. With today's highly mobile society, a usable transportation network is critical to everyday life as we know it.

Mechanical Engineering

"Mechanical engineering is basically the study of civil engineering systems that *move*," says Keri Sobolik, a mechanical engineer. Her husband, Steve, also a mechanical engineer, added, "Mechanical engineers do a lot of design work on dynamic systems. The profession really started by applying many of Newton's laws of physics to practical uses." Steve thinks that the mechanical engineering field was probably born as a result of warfare.

For as long as man has existed, there has been conflict in the world. Adversaries would square off and battle over many basic issues: territorial disputes, religious differences, and authoritative control. In order to defeat an enemy, a leader might rely on his latest technological advances to outperform the adversary's capabilities. Some notable technologies come to mind. The earliest long-range gun was probably developed by a budding mechanical engineer in the form of the large catapult. This moving mechanism consists of lever arms, gears, and other structural members that mechanical engineers might use to launch a payload. Hopefully, if an aerodynamicist (a closely related field discussed in the aerospace section of this chapter) had done his calculations properly, the payload would land in close proximity to the opposition.

The main focus of modern mechanical engineering is simply mechanical design. The mechanical design is applied to energy and movement of energy issues. Engineers typically design machinery of some sort that either produces, transmits, or uses power. The internal-combustion engine is designed to generate energy that is ultimately directed to do useful work, like moving a car. Jet engines are designed to supply enough thrust to lift an airplane off the ground. Nuclear reactors are designed to supply the electricity for many industrial uses.

The design responsibility of the mechanical engineer doesn't stop after the power is developed; the engineer must get the power where

```
┌─────────────────────────────┐
│   Mechanical Engineering    │
│       Energy Concept        │
└─────────────────────────────┘
        │           │           │
        ▼           ▼           ▼
   ┌────────┐  ┌──────────┐  ┌──────────┐
   │ Power  │─▶│  Power   │─▶│  Power   │
   │Generation│ │Transmission│ │Application│
   └────────┘  └──────────┘  └──────────┘
```

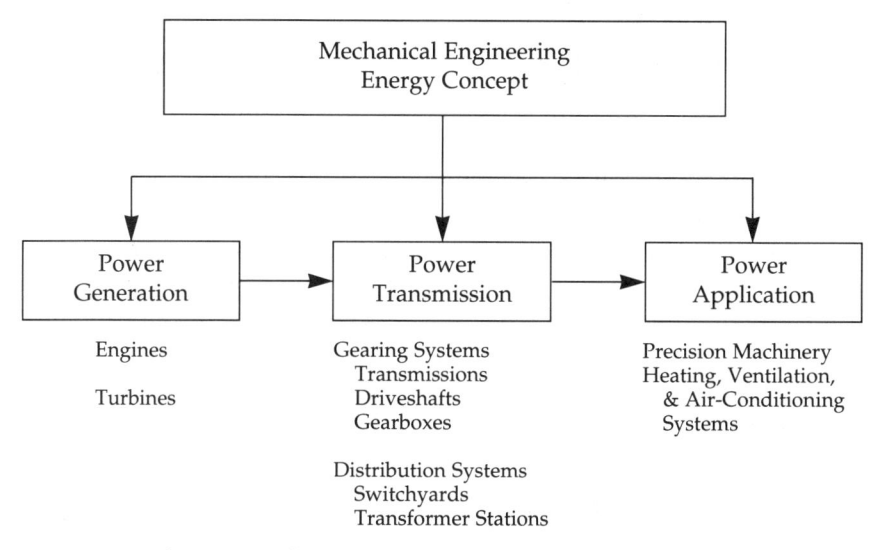

Engines	Gearing Systems	Precision Machinery
	Transmissions	Heating, Ventilation,
Turbines	Driveshafts	& Air-Conditioning
	Gearboxes	Systems
	Distribution Systems	
	Switchyards	
	Transformer Stations	

Figure 4-1. Definition of Mechanical Engineering Discipline

it's needed. This process is called transmission. An example is the automobile transmission. After the internal-combustion engine generates the power, it is moved through a transmission system to the wheels. This mechanism consists of a complex series of moving parts that must operate with precision timing. In the case of nuclear power, the mechanical engineer must design the power distribution system so that all users have power.

Machines that *use* power to do *work* are the mechanical engineer's responsibility as well. Most of us take this for granted, but can you recall life without heating or air-conditioning systems? The frigid winters of Alaska and the humid summers of Houston would be very different without these modern conveniences. The next time you go to the hardware store for whatever fix-it thing you need, think about the presses, lathes, and other machinery that made your item and you'll appreciate the value of a mechanical engineer.

Figure 4-1 summarizes these energy concepts (generation, transmission, and application) as they apply to the mechanical engineering field.

Transportation is another concept that mechanical engineers work with. However, transportation can mean different things to the mechanical engineer. Consider the movement of heat. To the mechanical engineer, this field is called *heat transfer*. It's the thermal sciences of chemical engineering as it applies to motion. Do you remember the old stand-alone radiators that heated homes a few decades ago? An engineer specializing in radiant heat designed those systems. In today's high-technology world, the heat transfer expert would understand the mechanism that heats the tiles on the space shuttle as it reenters the earth's atmosphere. It's also a common field of study in the defense industry.

Other specialties within mechanical engineering include manufacturing processes, computer-aided design (CAD) and computer-aided manufacturing (CAM), instrumentation and sensor technologies, and robotics. Steve Sobolik believes that "robotics is one of the fastest-growing professions in mechanical engineering." One area of robotics technology that will grow is hazardous- or toxic-waste cleanup and storage. Why risk a human life when a robot or other piece of machinery could easily do the job?

Chemical Engineering

"Chemical engineering is a cross between physical chemistry and mechanical engineering," says Stephanie Witkowski, a chemical engineer. Chemical engineers take small-scale chemical reactions in the lab and make them work on a large scale in support of a manufacturing process. Ultimately, the chemical engineer, like all engineers, produces a usable product for society.

Originally, the chemical engineer was largely responsible for the development of our nation's energy resources. The engineer might design processes or methods to extract, refine, or develop natural gas, crude oil, and other alternative fuels. Petroleum engineering grew out of this field of study. However, much of chemical engineering has evolved into manufacturing processes for the industrial production of chemicals. Stephanie says, "Many of the detergents, paints, fertilizers, and explosives were developed by a chemical engineer who made a large-scale process a reality. Many chemical engineers have gone to work at large chemical plants as process engineers."

Another common area of study is environmental engineering and waste management. Although some schools have this curriculum in the civil engineering department, many of the chemical engineering departments have taken on this field of study. The traditional environmental engineer examines separation techniques and chemical reactions necessary to break down waste into harmless by-products. Environmental engineers also study basic issues such as air pollution, hazardous-waste disposal, and groundwater contamination.

Two newer specialties exist within the chemical engineering discipline. The first involves the application of chemical engineering to the

```
                    ┌──────────────────────────────┐
                    │ Chemical Engineering Specialties │
                    └──────────────────────────────┘
```

Energy Resources	Industrial Production	Environment & Waste Management	Electronic Applications	Bio-Products
Crude Oil	Detergents	Chemical Waste Breakdown	Integrated Circuit Processes	Artificial Tissue
Natural Gas	Plastics	Waste Separation	Plating/	
Alternative Fuels	Explosives	Air Pollution	Pickling	
	Fertilizers			
	Wine Making			

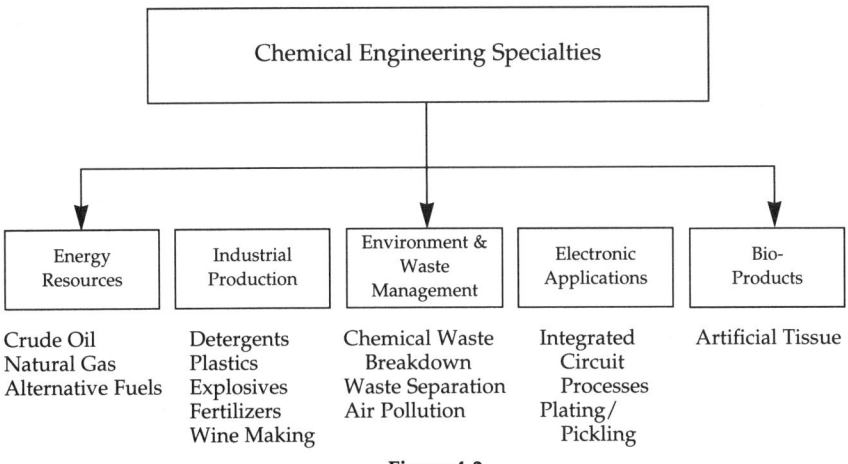

Figure 4-2

electronics fabrication industry. We all know that electrical engineers design items such as circuit boards. However, in the manufacturing process, many chemical issues often arise which inhibit the successful manufacturing of quality circuit boards. Stephanie says, "An example of this relationship between electronics and chemical engineering is the soldering of integrated circuits. This process is really unrelated to the electrical engineer's design, and the chemical engineer must solve any problems that arise in this process."

Walt Witkowski, who holds a doctorate in chemical engineering from the University of Texas at Austin, studied another relatively new specialty, genetically engineered bio-products. This field of study focuses on artificial tissue and how to replicate it synthetically. Walt researched and developed artificial muscle tissue, which has a wide variety of uses for people with deteriorated muscles and other tissue ailments.

Figure 4-2 shows the major specialties I've discussed in chemical engineering. See if you can't find something intriguing to you, and do a little research on your own!

Electrical Engineering

"Electrical engineering (EE) is by far the most common engineering discipline today," says Dave Kozlowski, who holds electrical engineering degrees from New Mexico State University and Purdue University. The Bureau of Labor Statistics verifies this, showing that the vast majority of all engineers graduate in this field. Why is it so popular?

Consider the law of supply and demand. Because our society is so dependent on electricity and electronic devices, it seems logical that there is a demand for electrical engineers. When was the last time you could do without your telephone, television, VCR, or microwave oven? Also, EE involves *cutting-edge* technologies. While cutting-edge bridges and cutting-edge machine tools may ultimately help society, the general public is more interested in how to make their everyday life a little easier. Electronic gadgetry fits the bill, and sells quite well, while cutting-edge bridges may not. Smart people with engineering tendencies, who want good-paying jobs, should look no further.

The EE profession is responsible for the research, design, development, and testing of a wide variety of electrical components, systems, or devices. Dave Kozlowski says, "The EE might design small components like the integrated circuit (IC). Another EE might use the IC design as a component of a more complex electronic control system in a large power plant. Communication systems and complex computer networks are fields that the EE might be involved in as well. As you can see, the electrical engineering field covers a lot of territory."

After surveying the literature on the electrical engineering professional society, the Institute of Electrical and Electronics Engineers (IEEE), I found thirty-seven societies and councils that form specialties within the profession. Several of the main specialties are listed below.[1]

a. The *circuits and devices* specialty involves the design and analysis of electrical circuitry and components. Basic circuit theory is studied, including analog and digital systems.

b. The *electromagnetics* specialty studies radar signal propagation and magnetic fields, as they apply to various technologies. The air traffic controller uses the tools and equipment derived from this specialty to safely direct airplanes.

c. The *power systems* field is perhaps the most traditional electrical engineering discipline. The power engineer designs and models generators and electrical transmission and distribution systems in conjunction with the mechanical engineer. Our society's industrial and household electrical codes are developed by this branch of EE.

d. The *control systems* field is responsible for the development of controlling algorithms for electronic and mechanical devices. The control engineer might work very closely with the mechanical engineer who specializes in robotics. Control systems are often used for large

---

[1] EE categories a–e are from Nicholas Basta, *Opportunities in Engineering Careers* (Lincolnwood, IL: VGM Career Horizons, 1990), pp. 47–48.

automated industrial systems, such as the automobile assembly line. Another application might involve an aerospace vehicle, such as controlling reentry bodies and other missile systems.

e. The *signal processing* specialty is responsible for the transmission and interpretation of electronic signals, usually through an analog or digital instrumentation measurement system. Electronic signals from acoustic, ultrasonic, or accelerometer devices are processed to provide useful data to the engineer. Clean, noise-free wave forms are desirable in all signal processing applications.

Recently, the study of *neural networks* has grown in popularity. It involves the training or programming of systems to imitate the neurons in the human brain. An example of the application of neural networks involves the recycling industry. A system is "trained" to sort materials into plastics, newspapers, and glass, perhaps by using a pattern recognition scheme. "This field has a lot of potential," says Dave. Maybe you could combine an interest in life sciences and engineering while studying this topic.

COMPUTER ENGINEERING

I contemplated making an entirely separate category for computer engineering, since it has nearly developed into a discipline of its own, but many schools still list the field under electrical engineering because much of the computer *hardware* design and development activities are really a specific application of electrical engineering technologies to computers. I would guess that the great majority of circuit boards in my laptop that I'm using to write this book were designed by an electrical engineer, rather than a computer engineer. However, you realize as well as I do that computers are an integral part of everyday life now, and the consumer will demand more efficient and faster systems. Computer engineers will no doubt evolve into a separate discipline as a result of this specific demand.

Computer engineers strive not only for faster, more efficient hardware designs but they also develop more efficient software systems. If a computer program is written in as few lines as possible, then the hardware disk storage and memory requirements won't be as taxing to the system. Efficiency in both hardware and software design is a goal that the computer engineer works toward. If you've enjoyed playing with computer hardware and software, this might be the field for you.

OTHER ELECTRICAL ENGINEERING SPECIALTIES

Although I have mentioned only seven of the thirty-seven IEEE societies and councils, there are others that might be just as interesting to you. The other thirty societies range from *dielectric and electrical insulation* to *information theory*. If you're interested in more information on these specialties, consult your local library or university or write the IEEE. (The addresses of all professional engineering societies are contained in the Appendix of this book.)

Mining Engineering

If you live in a major metropolitan area such as New York City, Washington, D.C., or San Francisco, you probably spend a great deal of time on the subway. The next time you ride through this vast maze of seemingly endless caverns, take note of the arch-type tunnel cross section that is probably steel- or concrete-lined. You probably assume that the tunnel roof or side walls won't cave in during your journey, and if the mining engineer has performed proper calculations and done adequate design work, you shouldn't have a care in the world as you wend your way through the holes in the ground.

Boring and tunneling operations for a subway system are only one aspect of mining engineering. The main thrust of the profession is to find and extract useful materials from the earth for industrial applications. To do this, the mining engineer must survey potential sites, along with the geological engineer, to determine the safest and most economical way to extract metals and minerals. Then the engineer devises a plan to create subsurface tunnels or surface pits to remove the material, using a wide variety of machines, tools, or blasting techniques. After the material is removed from the earth, a separation process purifies the material, discarding the undesirable geological residue. Gold, copper, silver, gypsum, and coal are just a few of the mining engineering end products.

Not only is the profession geared toward developing innovative mining techniques and equipment, but a greater emphasis has been placed on safety and environmental issues. The College of Mines at the University of Arizona created an engineering safety degree that was specifically developed for the mining industry, due in part to the number of fatalities in southern Arizona's coppermines.

New Kids on the Block

The next five engineering disciplines move us away from the more traditional engineering fields of study. Many of these fields were either specialties or combinations of traditional disciplines that eventually developed their own character. Table 4-2 summarizes the major categories and subcategories that we're about to explore.

Metallurgical Engineering

Bill Garcia, a retired metallurgical engineer, thinks there's a great need for metallurgical engineers in industry today, and he says there aren't many of them compared to engineers in other engineering disciplines. Nonetheless, it is an important engineering field. Quality materials for parts as varied as aircraft engine components and computer chips are developed and certified by the metallurgical engineer. The end product of a good metallurgical engineer's efforts is a safe, reliable material that operates and functions in all sorts of extreme conditions. You wouldn't want the skin of an airplane to catastrophically split at 40,000 feet!

The metallurgical engineer studies and develops traditional metals (such as aluminum and iron) and specialty metals (such as alloys and composites). Nonmetals (such as plastics and laminates) are studied by materials engineers, who have closely related curricula. Often this field concentrates on controlling the process of developing or making the material. This might include modifying casting, forging, or heat-treating techniques that ultimately produce improved material properties. Bill says, "Higher temperatures or conductive material capabilities are obtained by advanced processing techniques."

The engineer becomes involved in the entire manufacturing process for materials. "This includes setting the preheat temperatures and the number of reheats required to produce crack-free, high-quality parts in the forging industry," says Bill. It's best to avoid cracks in your car engine block!

If you're looking for a field with a lot of growth potential, consider this discipline.

Aerospace Engineering

"Aeronautical engineering was the genesis of aerospace engineering," says aerospace engineer Dennis Roach. Aeronautical engineering, or the study of "air-breathing" aircraft engines within the earth's atmo-

Table 4-2. Newer Engineering Disciplines

Metallurgical	Aerospace	Nuclear	Industrial	Systems
• Extractive Metallurgy	• Aerodynamics	• Reactor Research/Design	• Plant Layout	• Operations Research
• Alloying of Metals	• Structural	• Nuclear Fusion	• Ergonomics	• Simulations
• Effects of Processing Variables	• Propulsion	• Radiation Effects on Materials	• Operations Research	• Control Laws
	• Guidance and Control	• Medical Radiation Treatment	• Industrial Management	
	• Orbital Mechanics	• Radiation Health Physics	• Quality Control	

sphere, is now just one part of aerospace engineering. The field probably dates back at least to the days of Orville and Wilbur Wright, when man got serious about achieving human flight. It dates much further back when one considers the hot-air balloon as a method of flight.

Since the 1950s, aeronautical engineering was transformed into aerospace engineering, which includes flight vehicles such as missiles and spacecraft. Although the aerospace engineer is still intimately involved with the design of modern airplanes, the discipline now includes flight outside the earth's atmosphere. Dennis says, "It opened a whole new field of study—space flight, orbital mechanics, rocket propulsion, and the associated guidance and control issues."

He explains specialties within aerospace engineering, using a generic flight vehicle as an example. First, the aerospace engineer must *structurally* design the vehicle for flight. Next, the vehicle must have a *propulsion* system, such as rocket engines, to get it to where it's going. Then the engineer must understand *aerodynamic* characteristics. How does the craft react to flight within our atmosphere? How does the craft react once it's exo-atmospheric? What are the *vibration and flutter* environments that the vehicle will encounter?

In conjunction with the in-flight aerodynamic environments, the vehicle must be able to maneuver. The aerospace engineer designs a *guidance and control system* that allows the craft to adapt or adjust to the environments that nature has supplied. The guidance and control systems sense an environment, such as aerodynamic flutter or vibration, and initiate appropriate action to correct the effect through a control loop/feedback logic circuit.

If the vehicle is launched into space, an aerospace engineer who has special training in *orbital mechanics* is required. The specialty involves the prediction of vehicle movement, such as a satellite as it orbits the earth, or moves to other locations in outer space. Think about this field of study the next time you watch the space shuttle orbit the earth.

Steve Doerr, who holds a Ph.D. in aerospace engineering, explained his interest in the field. "The aerospace field intrigued me because the aircraft or spacecraft was in motion, which meant that the forces and responses were time-dependent. This dynamic training is useful in a wide range of applications, such as earthquake motion studies, combustion phenomena, and impact processes (bullets and other projectiles). The field is rapidly expanding in these other applications." The aerospace engineer does not always work in the aerospace industry, and, as you can see, the opportunities are quite varied.

Nuclear Engineering

Samantha Lapin, who has bachelor's and master's degrees in nuclear engineering, had this to say:

> In the broadest sense, the nuclear engineer studies various aspects associated with gains derived from the use of nuclear energy. Much of the focus is geared toward the nuclear reactor, which usually acts as a furnace to heat water. The heated water is then converted to steam, which drives a turbine for a generator. Ultimately, the generator produces electricity. The power from the nuclear reactor is used for both terrestrial and space systems.
>
> Additional studies for the nuclear engineering student include nuclear fusion, radiation effects on materials, radiation medical treatment, and radiation health physics. Because a lot of emphasis is placed on the nuclear reactor, the nuclear engineer must be firmly grounded in all of the different aspects concerning its implementation, which includes thermal transport, thermal hydraulics, materials, structures, power conditioning (electronics), and nuclear waste. Universities in the United States do not provide any instruction in the area of nuclear energy used for military applications. The military, however, does offer courses in these areas for its own employees and industry affiliates.

Industrial Engineering

When I asked Pauline Goolsby, who has a bachelor's degree in industrial engineering from the University of Texas at El Paso, about her field of study, she said, "The curriculum is really geared toward engineering management and quality control issues as they relate to industrial and manufacturing processes."

The industrial engineer (IE) has a broad background in major fields such as electrical, mechanical, and civil engineering. This curriculum gives the industrial engineer the necessary background tools to *manage* large industrial processes. Additional IE coursework emphasizes efficient, quality operations.

"Production layout techniques are taught after a series of basic courses such as quality control, engineering economics, and accounting are completed. Special areas such as operations research, ergonomics, and queuing are also taught in the IE school," says Pauline. Operations research is the study of methodologies designed to optimize a procedure, while ergonomics is the engineering study of human behavior. Queuing involves the prediction of when to optimally perform an operation.

The tools that an industrial engineer develops in school can be applied to a wide variety of activities, including hospital operations (personnel work-flow processes), fabrication plants (machinery layout), and inventory processes (information flow). Pauline's industrial engineering experience involved the car engine manufacturing business, with emphasis on parts assembly. She mentioned that the industrial engineer must always seek the most cost-effective solution, which in her case involved the assembly of parts in Juárez, Mexico. "It was a simple matter of less costly resources in Juárez," says Pauline. Sometimes the industrial engineering solutions are not high-technology solutions, but rather a simple, efficient use of human resources.

Systems Engineering

Gregg Skow, who has a bachelor's degree in systems engineering, calls systems engineering a broad-based field that develops, uses, or applies different methodologies to solve problems. Systems engineers (SEs) analyze large complex problems, developing models and *simulations* to predict or optimize activities. A good example of an SE application is the airline scheduling business. A mathematical model of decisions and choices is developed, such as flight takeoff and landing times. System constraints are put on the problem, like aircraft speeds and weather conditions, to identify the boundary conditions. Changes in the system are assessed by varying key parameters, such as uncertainty in aircraft mechanical problems that cause delays. These aberrations are modeled to prevent the system from failing (i.e., takeoff and landing gridlock) when such events occur.

Operations research is also a specialty within SE. Many military decisions are modeled as a result of this field of study. Battlefield exercises, war-gaming efforts, and sortie requirements are determined by SE methodologies that are used to train military officers.

Gregg said that some of the SE coursework was ill-defined while he was in school, since the field is so new. As a result, he spent lots of time taking electrical and computer engineering classes. For example, another SE specialty involves the study of *control systems*, similar to the EE specialty mentioned earlier. The SE studies feedback and filtering techniques from a system perspective. "Many of our large communication systems take advantage of this specialty," says Gregg. There will be plenty of good opportunities for this field of study in the future.

Other Disciplines

I have not reviewed all disciplines. In some cases, the discipline is a subset or combination of one of the fields that we've already discussed. In other cases, the field is an advanced specialty that is studied in graduate school. Nonetheless, it is important to recognize some of these specialties, and if you want more information, consult your local university or write to one of the professional organizations listed in the Appendix.

Agricultural Engineering (Ag E) obviously involves the engineering of the food production industry. The Ag E might be involved in special equipment design (planting or harvesting), using mechanical engineering methods. The profession also deals with economical and efficient uses of resources, such as water (irrigation techniques) and land reclamation.

Biomedical Engineering is the application of engineering techniques to life sciences. Major engineering fields are used to solve medical problems. The biomedical engineer might be involved in artificial limb design (mechanical), pacemaker development (mechanical and electrical), or synthetic tissue research (chemical).

Ceramics Engineering is really an element of metallurgical engineering. Ceramic materials such as glass (china) and clay (pottery) were developed by this profession. A more recent specialty involves the development of special thermal insulating coatings for space vehicles.

Engineering Mathematics and *Engineering Physics* are exactly what their titles imply—the application of physics and mathematical theory to facilitate the solution of engineering problems.

Geological Engineering is an element of mining, metallurgical, and chemical engineering. If you like rocks and rock formations, then this field is for you.

Manufacturing Engineering is a combination of mechanical, electrical, and industrial engineering applied to the study of efficient industrial processes. This specialty is often studied at the graduate level.

Possibilities Within Your Chosen Discipline

The mode of operation as an engineer can vary greatly within a discipline. Would you rather develop equations for joint connections between beams and columns, or would you rather research the issues involved? Would you rather analyze an existing joint that someone else designed, or design it yourself? Would you like to build a scaled model of the joint and test it to failure in the laboratory? All of these engineering modes are not always so compartmentalized; in many cases one engineer or team of engineers might be responsible for developing theoretical equations for certain phenomena, as well as design, analysis, and test for practical applications. Certainly, these engineering functions and responsibilities are interrelated and dependent on one another. So let me give you a feel for these more traditional modes of operation.

Many engineering firms speak of RDT&E when they put proposals together. That is, when they bid on a project, such as the development of new hardware or processes, they must consider the cost of *research, development, test,* and *evaluation* to produce the product. If the product is completely new and not available "off the shelf," a lot of research is involved. With many new technologies, mathematical models and governing equations must be established by the *researcher* before any of the work can be done.

Next, a team of *designers* uses the tools developed in research to start thinking about what the product might look like. The designers brainstorm and quickly develop sketches or "cartoons" of their thoughts. Then the team eliminates the ideas that won't work or are outrageously expensive. With the remaining ideas, the designers get serious about putting pencil to paper (or, in today's world, fingers to computer keyboards), assimilating details such as material specifications or system constraints.

Once the design has enough detail, predictions are made concerning the robustness of the design. A team of *analysts* assumes responsibility for pieces of the design and runs computer models or simulations of the hardware in its predicted environment. Ultimately, the analysts determine the integrity of the design.

Although the computer analysis gives indications of design integrity, the mathematical models and governing equations are not always exact solutions to the problem. In most cases, simplifying assumptions are made, allowing the analyst to make predictions. Hence, the design process moves to the test and evaluation phase. In some instances, scaled models or other mock-ups are simulated in the laboratory under realistic environments. Measurements are taken to assimilate system performance, and the evaluation of data completes the laboratory work. As a result of the test and evaluation phase, modifications to the design or process are usually proposed. The RDT&E concept is a process in which design engineers, analysts, and test engineers all have overlapping duties.

It is customary in the engineering field for all engineers to operate in one or more of the RDT&E modes mentioned above. However, as the engineer becomes more experienced, knowledgeable, and comfortable with his profession, he may choose to move into management, sales, or private consulting. When he moves into these positions, he combines his technical know-how with his people skills, using a combination of talents that may not be as scientifically "hard-core." As

Number of Engineers per Discipline

Employment (thousands)

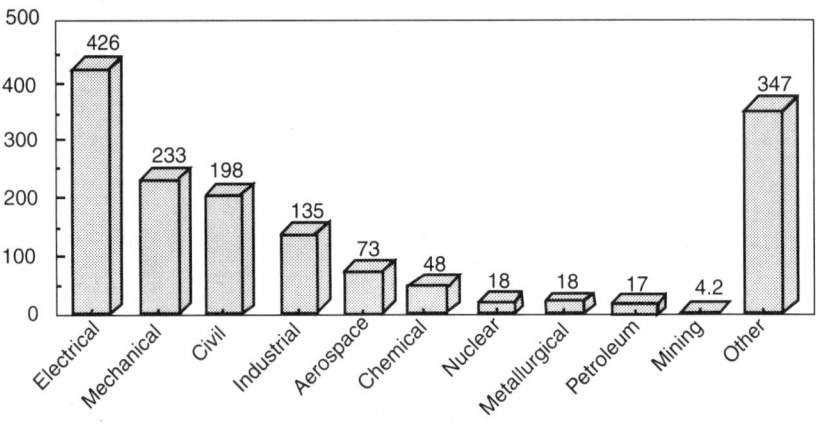

Discipline	Employment
Electrical	426
Mechanical	233
Civil	198
Industrial	135
Aerospace	73
Chemical	48
Nuclear	18
Metallurgical	18
Petroleum	17
Mining	4.2
Other	347

Figure 4-3   Source: *Occupational Outlook Handbook*

Ingrid Eng, who works in the civil engineering consulting business, says, "When you become a consultant or a manager, it is expected that you're technically competent. And it is imperative that you like to work with the public, whether it is another contractor, a government worker, or a junior engineer."

Still Confused?

With the large amount of information just presented to you, hopefully there was some topic or field that intrigued you. The Bureau of Labor Statistics recently compiled the number of engineers employed by discipline (shown in Figure 4-3). By far, the most popular engineering field today is electrical engineering. Mechanical, civil, and industrial engineering follow in second, third, and fourth place, respectively. Although this chart is geared toward employment statistics, it also highlights the current demand by engineering discipline.

Mechanical engineer Keri Sobolik and I agree that the smartest thing to do is to pick one of the major engineering disciplines if you don't have a strong affinity for any particular field. As a case in point, Keri says, "Although petroleum engineering is still a popular field, it isn't as popular as it was a few years ago. This is due primarily to the bust in the oil industry in recent years. Consequently, the ever popular petroleum engineer was no longer in demand, and many had a hard time finding jobs." Thus, pick one of the major four traditional fields —electrical, mechanical, civil, or chemical—and you can't go wrong! They'll always be in demand.

· 5 ·

WHICH ENGINEERING SCHOOL TO CHOOSE

The Sky Is the Limit

We're all under external constraints and limitations. I can think of a lot of reasons why I *didn't* choose an engineering school other than the University of Arizona. Here are a few of my thoughts from about ten years ago when I was just coming out of high school.

- Out-of-state schools and private institutions are simply not affordable.
- I don't want to move from my hometown.
- My ACT or SAT scores might limit my entrance to certain schools.
- The city where the school of my first choice is located is too big or too small for me.
- I don't have any friends or family in the vicinity of the schools I'm looking at.
- The military or religious schools are not for me.
- Community colleges are very limited in their curriculum.

As you review this chapter, keep an open mind. Break down the barriers for a moment. Forget about the school requirements, especially money and ACT or SAT test scores. Entertain the thought that no school is unrealistic for you. What about the Massachusetts Institute of Technology (MIT)? What about Stanford University? What about the Air Force Academy? Why would you attend any of these institutions? Why wouldn't you attend any of these institutions? Let's approach this discussion from the scientific viewpoint. We'll develop a hypothesis, which will be a list of candidate schools by type. Then we'll set up an experiment by gathering data and information, assimilating it, and drawing a conclusion by choosing the school that suits your unique interests and needs. After all, you're going to spend the rest of your life (perhaps) in this career, and you want the best foundation to build on.

The "Ski" Is the Limit

It's no secret that I like to ski; in fact, it dominated my thinking when I was in high school. Unfortunately, my guiding principle in choosing an engineering school was not "the sky is the limit," but "the ski is the limit." Interestingly enough, when I asked some of my colleagues about their reasons for choosing their engineering school, I found that I wasn't alone in my thinking. John Patterson, who is also a civil engineer, says:

> I almost ended up in aerospace engineering and even preregistered for it at Arizona State University (ASU). But when I also preregistered for civil engineering at the University of Arizona, I found out that the freshman class load was much lighter there. My classes were scheduled at ASU from 8 a.m. to 5 p.m. every day with no break for lunch. It made for an easy decision to attend the University of Arizona, one that I now believe was the correct one despite the logic I used at the time.

As you can see, John Patterson and I could have benefited from some good "inside" advice in choosing our schools, even though things turned out O.K. for both of us. Remember, although outside activities are important to your overall educational experience, you're going to school to get the best engineering education that you can. Don't worry yet about the class times, ski areas, or other minor details in making this decision.

You might recall that in Chapter 3 I emphasized the importance of good planning in your engineering career development process. It's now time to actually *develop a plan* to help you choose a school. I'll guarantee that your plan will be more substantial than my whimsical notion of *skiing my way to success in the Rocky Mountains of Colorado*.

Engineering School Options

When I thought about all of the options available to young students today, I was almost tempted to do it all over again myself, differently of course. Consider getting your engineering degree in one or more of these "modes."

- Primarily Technical Schools (MIT, Virginia Polytechnic Institute)
- Military Academies (U.S. Air Force Academy, U.S. Military Academy, U.S. Naval Academy)

- Religious Institutions (University of Notre Dame, Brigham Young University)
- State Schools (University of Southern California)
- Private Institutions (Stanford University, Cornell University)
- Community Colleges
- Correspondence Courses
- Closed-Circuit Television
- Company-Sponsored Programs
- Overseas
- Study on a Boat
- Predominantly Minority Schools (Historically Black Colleges and Universities)
- Predominantly Gender-Specific Schools (Virginia Military Institute)

Although it is unlikely that you will try all of the above modes of engineering education, it is quite possible that you might come into contact with more than one as you wend your way down the engineering path. As an example, I attended state schools at the University of Arizona and Purdue University; a company-sponsored engineering program at Sandia National Laboratories; a closed-circuit television course in finite element analysis at Indiana University and Purdue University; and computer courses at Pima Community College in Tucson. Unfortunately, I've never had formal training overseas, although I'd like to. Sometime I'd like to have a hands-on experience in ancient Egyptian structures. Better yet, I'd like to study the rudimentary construction methods that built St. Peter's Basilica in Rome in a few hundred years!

I've heard of engineers who entered the workforce with a basic engineering degree from a military academy and pursued advanced specialty engineering degrees at a private institution such as Stanford University, or a technical school such as the Virginia Polytechnic Institute. I've even heard of people who spent many years getting their engineering degree and a liberal arts degree of some sort. The permutations and combinations are quite varied, and the more exposure you have to different ways of thinking, the better. Don't limit yourself yet; keep your options open for the time being.

Let's Do Some Research

The best way to educate yourself about schools is to do some research first. I'll guide you through the process by asking you a few questions, and provide you with a School Facts work sheet for you to complete.

The result of this exercise should be a broad list of schools for you to consider.

Question 1. What are your engineering education goals? Write them in the space provided.

Insight to Question 1. You must begin this process by summarizing, in words and on paper, what your objective is in your engineering education. It might be fairly simple such as "a sound engineering education at a major university in my home state" or it might be more complex, such as "an engineering degree combined with an in-depth study of military history from a small private school." It's O.K. to make this statement far-reaching and next to impossible—you can always modify it later if you need to. Remember, the sky is the limit!

Write your engineering education goals here.

Question 2. What engineering school *issues or parameters* are important to you? Why?

Insight to Question 2. Here you might consider issues such as engineering school size—does it matter if it's big or small? Student-to-professor ratios—do you want individual attention from professors? Quality of the specific field of study—is the school ranked among the top ten schools in the nation? Types of engineering degrees available—do you want a specific degree in engineering physics? Not all of these parameters may be important to you. I didn't care about the engineering school's size, as long as the student-to-professor ratio was low. I was interested in civil engineering, which allowed a broad variety of engineering school options for me.

Write your response to the question about the engineering issues and parameters here.

56   *Majoring in Engineering*

Question 3. Do you have any special interests that you must consider in your decision?

Insight to Question 3. This may not apply to you, but if you're seriously considering a double major (engineering and economics, for example), you may want to note this fact. Or you may have a special skill or talent (musical or athletic, for example) which might influence your decision. It could be that your religious beliefs play a role in your decision to pick a particular school as well. If you write something in this section, make sure it doesn't fall into my "ski is the limit" category. I'm sure that you have a lot of outside interests like anybody else, but make certain that they're important enough to influence your engineering education decision.

Write your special interests here.

Question 4. Do you have any special needs that you must consider in making your engineering education decision?

Insight to Question 4. Not everyone will have a response to this question either, but it could be a major factor in your decision-making process. If you're physically handicapped or disabled, and you have special needs, you obviously want to consider this in your selection of schools. Perhaps you have special hearing problems that require a sign-language interpreter. Or you may have a special medical requirement. Perhaps you must be near a major metropolitan center with a dialysis machine, or you must be near a heart specialist.

Special needs might be in the form of family issues too. Do you require special child-care facilities or married-student housing? Be sure to consider these issues before making your decision.

Write your response to the special needs question.

After putting pencil to paper on the above questions, let's generate a table of information, the School Facts work sheet, to organize your data in a compact form. First, in Table 5-1, I will provide examples and discussion on how to use the information. Then in Table 5-2 you will have a chance to fill in your own information. It may even be convenient for you to make several copies of Table 5-2 before you write in it.

Sources of Information, Examples, and Discussion on How to Use Table 5-1 (by column)

To complete Table 5-2, consult your school career guidance center, whether it be high school, technical or vocational school, or university or college. If they don't have this information, try the local public library.

1. *Peterson's Four Year Colleges 1995,* Princeton, NJ, Peterson's Guides. Nearly three inches thick, this book contains information on almost 2,000 colleges and universities. It details individual school statistics such as size, location, and enrollment, as well as majors, admission requirements, and special programs. It also provides a lot of good general information.

2. *Lovejoy's College Guide,* edited by Charles T. Straughn II and Barbarasue Lovejoy Straughn, Englewood Cliffs, NJ, Prentice Hall, 1991. An excellent source for cross-referencing college information.

3. *Profiles of American Colleges,* Hauppauge, NY, Barron's Educational Series, 1991. This book has a broad range of information that will allow you to accurately complete the table. The information even states the percentage of a campus that's accessible to physically handicapped students. It's another excellent source for cross-referencing college information.

4. *Rugg's Recommendations on the Colleges,* Frederick E. Rugg, Haydenville, MA, Rugg Recommendations, 1988–89. This book provides information on the best departments in universities and colleges. The data was gathered by polling students at 500 colleges and universities. You can find a listing of the engineering schools that have been highly recommended by other engineering students.

5. *The Gourman Report: A Rating of Undergraduate Programs in American and International Universities,* Dr. Jack Gourman, Los Angeles, CA, National Education Standards, 1989. This book rates, by engineering discipline, the top schools in the country and the world. It's another good cross-reference report for your database of information.

6. *Peterson's Two Year Colleges 1995,* Princeton, NJ, Peterson's Guides. If you want to start your education at a two-year institution, you may

Table 5-1. Example Engineering School Facts Chart

School	Type/Accred.	Size	Stud./Prof. Ratio	Engineering Disciplines	Engr. School Ranking	Special Interests?	Special Needs?	Comments
School 1								
School 2								
School 3 (Hometown)	Community/No	20,000	12:1	Engineering Technology	Not Applicable	Good Laboratories	Can Accommodate	Good Follow-on
School 4								
School 5 (Houston)	State/Yes	5,600	Unknown	CE, ChemE, EE, IE, ME	None in Top 50	Good English Dept.	Can Accommodate	Out of State
School 6 (London)	Private/Yes	16,000	25:1	CE, EE, ME, ChemE	Unknown	Religious Instruction	Married-Student Housing	Continue Active Duty
School 7								
School 8 (New Jersey)	Military/Yes	8,000	10:1	General Engineering	Top 15 in Most	ROTC Available	None	Career Military
School 9 (Los Angeles)	Technical/Yes	30,000	15:1	CE, EE, IE, ME, SE	Most in Top 15	Good Athletics	90% Access to Campus	Further Study
School 10								
Summary Information								

want to consider reviewing this book. It details information similar to that of the four-year guide listed above.

7. *The Macmillan Guide to Correspondence Study*, compiled and edited by Modoc Press, Inc., New York, Macmillan Publishing Company, 1990. Many major universities have departments for independent study. You may want to supplement your engineering education by taking a correspondence course or two. This "how to" book contains details on taking advantage of this educational opportunity.

8. *The Multicultural Student's Guide to Colleges: What Every African-American, Asian-American, Hispanic, and Native American Applicant Needs to Know about America's Top Schools,* Robert Mitchell, New York, Noonday Press, 1993. A critical look at what more than 200 colleges have to offer students of color—both socially and academically.

After you've located a few good sources of information, complete Table 5-2. Don't forget to review your responses to the questions given earlier in this chapter. Here are some examples and insights on completing the table. You'll want to consult this discussion quite often as you complete Table 5-2.

Column 1. School. I suggest that you choose ten schools to analyze.

Column 2. Type/Accred. Record the type of institution as well as its accreditation standing with the Accreditation Board for Engineering and Technology.

Insights on Type. Record the type of school here. The following are the major types of schools to choose from:

- Primarily Technical Schools (Technical). These schools specialize in scientific curricula such as engineering. Many of the nation's top-rated engineering schools fall in this category (e.g., MIT, Virginia Polytechnic Institute).
- Military Academies (Military). These schools are primarily officer-training schools that offer various disciplines including engineering studies. They often have highly rated engineering programs (e.g., U.S. Air Force Academy, U.S. Military Academy, U.S. Naval Academy). You may also want to consider any service obligations you might have after graduation. (You may be obligated to serve several years of active duty.)
- Religious Institutions (Religious). Religious institutions offer studies in the engineering field too. Examples include the University of Notre Dame and Brigham Young University.

- State Schools (State). These schools are usually subsidized by state and federal funds, and in some cases are land-grant institutions. They offer many engineering programs, but specific disciplines may vary by institution. Examples include Purdue University and Oklahoma State University.
- Private Institutions (Private). Private institutions are schools that are not subsidized by federal, state, or local funding. Rather, independent entities (private corporations, student tuitions, and other endowments) serve as the school's primary sources of funding. Typically, these schools are more expensive than state schools, and the quality of the education they offer can be stellar. Examples of private institutions with engineering curricula include Stanford University and Cornell University.
- Community Colleges (Community). Most community colleges are affiliated with smaller, local communities. Some offer degrees in engineering technology, which might serve as a basis for getting your regular engineering degree. Also, some students take many of their basic college courses at a community college, and eventually transfer some of their credits to other colleges. This is usually an inexpensive option compared to four years of university costs.

Insights on Accreditation (Yes or No). The school's accreditation standing is important, because it shows that the institution meets basic engineering educational standards. These standards are recognized and accepted nationwide. If you cannot find a source of information that states whether or not the engineering program is accredited, write or call the following organization for more information:

Accreditation Board for Engineering and Technology, Inc.
345 East 47th Street
New York, NY 10017-2397
(212) 705-7000

Think twice about attending an institution that is not accredited, unless it's a community college that has transferable credits to an engineering-accredited university.

Column 3. Size (number of undergraduate students—designated as Small, Medium, or Large). The size or number of undergraduate students can be an important factor to some people. This *might* give an indication of the amount of personalized attention that you receive in school; however, it *might* be an indication of a broader (or narrower) set of different experiences that you may want to expose yourself to. Consider using these numbers of undergraduate students for marking this column of information:

Small: less than 5,000 undergraduate students
Medium: between 5,000 and 15,000 undergraduate students
Large: more than 15,000 undergraduate students

Column 4. Stud./Prof. Ratio. (XX:Y). In answering this question Y is the number of professors (assume 1) and XX is the number of students to one professor. This information is readily available in the sources listed above, and it is a strong indication of the amount of personalized attention you might get from your professors. I can't emphasize enough the importance of developing one-on-one relationships with your technical or engineering professors. There will be many things that you don't understand or you need clarification on, and your professor's personalized attention is the key to your success in many courses. Obviously, the lower the ratio, the better the personalized attention will be. Here are some rough numbers for you to consider:

Ratios less than 10:1. You'll be in small, intimate classes where you'll get a lot of individualized attention from the professors.
Ratios between 10:1 and 20:1. You'll be in medium-size classes where you'll get some individualized attention if you seek it out on your own. Otherwise, you may just be "another ship in the ocean, floating around." Most schools, especially state schools, fall into this category.
Ratios more than 20:1. You'll be in large classes where the professor's attention may not be individually focused on any single person's time. Even if you seek out individualized attention, the professor might simply be overwhelmed with the number of students in a class. Many introductory courses would fall in this category, and you need to make sure that you don't get lost in the shuffle at a large school.

Column 5. Engineering Disciplines (use the abbreviations listed below). Having read Chapter 4 on engineering disciplines, you should have an idea about your particular interests. Most schools have the traditional engineering disciplines, but many don't have the nontraditional disciplines. Be sure to review this information carefully for each school.

List of Abbreviations for Engineering Disciplines

Traditional Engineering Disciplines	Nontraditional Engineering Disciplines
Electrical (EE)	Industrial (IE)
Mechanical (ME)	Aerospace (ASE)
Civil (CE)	Nuclear (NE)
Chemical (ChemE)	Metallurgical (MetE)
Mining (MnE)	Systems (SE)

Column 6. Engr. School Ranking (scored as a number/total number of schools with the discipline). Although this information is somewhat subjective, you should get a feel for the quality of the engineering discipline as viewed by other knowledgeable people. Those people include students, former students, and educational professionals who keep data on curricula indicators. You should review multiple sources of information with different viewpoints. Even though a particular engineering school may not rank in the upper half of some survey, it does not mean that you'll get a bad education. According to *The Gourman Report*, for example, the University of Arizona undergraduate civil engineering program is ranked number 52 of the 54 schools shown. And I felt I got a good education. Note, however, that *The Gourman Report* ranks the leading institutions for civil engineering programs. There are others, I assume, that are not shown, which rank below these 54 institutions. Although employers tend to favor hiring from highly ranked schools, this score is not grounds to discount a school in your selection process. An education is what you make of it, and employers want good engineers for employees, not good schools.

Column 7. Special Interests? You should record whether or not the school serves your *serious* special interest here (i.e., those that don't fall into my "ski is the limit" category). Some examples might include religious instruction, professional music development (vocal, instrumental), military involvement, artistic talents (drawing, painting, ballet, etc.), sporting activities (football, softball, hockey, soccer, etc.).

Column 8. Special Needs? This column might include special handicapped services, married-student housing, child-care facilities, or specific medical or health facilities.

Column 9. Comments. Perhaps there is some other bit of information that you feel is important for your consideration.

Examples in Table 5-1

To provide further insights for your database of information on engineering schools, I will review and discuss the sample information in Table 5-1 as a hypothetical thought process that you might go through.

- School 3 is located in your hometown, which might allow you to live at home. It's a local community college that offers a two-year degree in engineering technology. This will enable you to get a taste of engineering without going full-bore at a major university or college. However, you would need to continue your engineering education at a university that will accept the credits you've earned at the local college. It has a somewhat large student population with moderate student-to-teacher ratios; you'll have to seek individualized student-teacher interactions on your own. One specific feature of the engineering curricula that intrigued you was the excellent quality of laboratory facilities and instruction at the school. The hands-on experiences are important to you at this institution.
- School 5 is located out of your home state in Houston. It's a state school that is relatively small, and the exact student-to-professor ratio is not available, but you suspect that it's a fairly good ratio. The school offers the traditional engineering disciplines, with a few specialty or nontraditional engineering disciplines as well. Unfortunately, none of the engineering schools are ranked in the top 50 or so schools. Because you're interested in technical writing, the English department is important to you. The school is known for its good-quality English department.
- School 6 is a fairly large school located in London, England. It has a high student-to-professor ratio, which means that you're going to vie with other students for the professor's attention. It offers only the traditional engineering disciplines, but it will allow you to continue your active-duty service in the U.S. military. The broad set of experiences in a foreign country are valuable to you, and may be useful in landing an engineering job. It also offers studies in the religious field that you're interested in.
- School 8 is a moderate-size military academy that is accredited with the Board for Engineering and Technology. It offers broad engineering studies; many are listed as top-ranked engineering schools in the country. After a career as a military officer, the engineering studies and experiences in the military will easily allow you to get a good civilian job.

- School 9 is a large technically oriented school in Los Angeles. It offers a variety of engineering disciplines, and the breadth of the institution will enable you to explore more options and alternatives in your engineering career. Because you are a tennis player, the quality of the athletic department is also important to you. Nearly all of the engineering departments are highly rated by the sources that you've consulted.

Be sure to complete your input to Table 5-2 now. Ignore the summary row for the time being.

Assimilating the Data

In a format similar to the examples I've just provided (review pages 59 to 62), write a paragraph or two on each of the schools in Table 5-2. If after you've written the paragraph you want to list the advantages and disadvantages of each school, then do so. It's important for you to write this information on paper, because it will force you to think carefully about each point that you're considering in this decision.

Another convenient way to assimilate this information is to use the summary row in Table 5-2. For each column in the table, write a few words in the corresponding summary box that highlights what is most important to you. Look back to your answers to Questions 1–4 for some key words. For example, my insight to Question 1 (earlier in this chapter) hypothetically stated that my goal was to get "an engineering degree with an in-depth study of military history from a small private school." In the summary box for Column 2, I might write "Private or Military." In Column 3, I might write "Small."

After you've entered the summary information for all nine columns of the table, highlight the boxes which meet your goals with a yellow marker. For example, if I wrote "Private or Military" in the summary box for Column 2, I would review all of the information in Column 2 and highlight those boxes that matched Private or Military. In the case of Table 5-1, I would highlight the box corresponding to School 6 and Column 2, as well as School 8 and Column 2. I'll tell you what all of the yellow boxes mean later, if you haven't figured it out already!

Financial Considerations

I've avoided the subject of finances until now because I felt that the quality of your engineering education and your college experience was far more important than money. However, financial considerations are

Table 5-2. Engineering School Facts Chart

School	Type/Accred.	Size	Stud./Prof. Ratio	Engineering Disciplines	Engr. School Ranking	Special Interests?	Special Needs?	Comments
Summary Information								

the reality of the world that we live in, and it would be foolish not to explore the costs of the ten or so schools that you've chosen.

Rich Engstrom, my nuclear engineering colleague, had this to say:

> After high school, I couldn't afford college, so I went into the Air Force and worked on airplanes. . . . I was four years in before my job would allow me to take college courses. . . . At the time I happened to be in England and I had an opportunity to take night classes at Cambridge. . . . My courses were structured along a path which would allow me to compete in an Air Force degree program in engineering.

Rich's experiences were somewhat extreme. He felt that he couldn't afford college at all, and the Air Force was the best opportunity to get an education. His story was very similar to those of other engineers, including mine. Consider Jon Rogers's story.

> A recruiter from Iowa State for the College of Engineering came to my high school senior algebra/pre-calculus class. He said that engineering science was the hardest major and I wanted a challenge. Not only that, but in-state tuition was affordable.

Although Rich's and Jon's choices were guided primarily by financial considerations, they felt that they had quality engineering experiences. However, I would not recommend that this be your only criterion for choosing an engineering school.

Here's an inspirational quotation from *The Scholarship Book*, by Daniel J. Cassidy and Michael J. Alves, one of the many books that I'll recommend for college financial information. The title of the paragraph is "Investigate the Information."

> Don't say you can't apply [for financial aid] because your parents earn too much money; 80% of the private sector does not require that you submit a financial statement or prove need. Don't think the deadlines for applying occur only in the fall of the school year; the private sector deadlines are passing daily, because they are set to coincide with the tax year or organizational meeting dates. Don't feel grades are the only criteria for an award; many application questions deal with personal, occupational, educational background, organizational affiliation, talent and ethnic origins. Don't be concerned with age; 42% of all college students are over the age

of 25, and many organizations are interested in the re-entry student and the mid-career development student. The Business and Professional Woman's Foundation awards hundred of scholarships to applicants who must be over the ages of 25 and 35. There is even a scholarship at San Francisco State University for students over the age of 60.

In considering your choice of schools, don't let the price tag scare you off. It's probably more common than not that students finish their education *in debt*, and some of the costs can be defrayed by other sources. Your college financial support falls into five simple categories. The first is private support from you, your family, and savings. The second is from grants based usually upon need. The third is from scholarships based on achievement, merit, or other specific qualifications. The fourth is from low-interest educational loans, and the fifth is from outside employment opportunities.

I was probably the exception rather than the norm, because I came out of my engineering educational experience completely debt-free. It really wasn't a goal of mine; it just happened that way. If I had it to do over again, I wouldn't let money scare me off as it did during my late teenage years. My undergraduate financing was a combination of three of the five financial support systems mentioned above. The first was my parents. They allowed me to live at home (free rent and food) as long as I was accomplishing something in school. The second was a minority engineering scholarship based on achievement and ethnicity. I was a Hispanic with a reasonably good GPA, and I had to maintain a B average to keep my scholarship. During my upperclassman years, I received another scholarship that was awarded for my scholastic achievements. These awards covered nearly all of the tuition, books, and fees throughout my undergraduate years. The final source of financial support was part-time work. During all of my undergraduate years, I worked part-time as a busboy in an ice-cream store/restaurant and as a chemical lab technician in a metal-plating shop. The money I received from my outside work went toward my transportation and entertainment expenses. (Yes, college students have a life too, beyond studies.)

Other people did not have it as easy (financially) as I did during my undergraduate years. The majority of college students who don't qualify for scholarships or grants get student loans of some sort. The bad news about student loans is that they need to be paid back after you're out of school.

Sources of Financial Data and Financial Aid Information

I wish that I had gone to the local public library when I was considering financing my education. I am amazed at the financial information available to students today. Since the purpose of this chapter is to concentrate on the quality of your engineering education, I am going to refer you to several excellent financial data sources for the ten or so schools you've selected in Table 5-2, instead of going through a lot of specifics here. Many of the sources have detailed tabular data by school on tuition, books, fees, room and board, and financial aid packages. Some of the sources even have convenient work sheets to compute your eligibility for grants, loans, and scholarships. Take advantage of this information, as well as any information you can obtain from your career guidance center at the nearest local high school, college, or university. As *The Scholarship Book* puts it: "Many . . . private endowments go unclaimed because qualified students do not know they exist! . . . The money is there; billions go unclaimed . . . The student loses every advantage by not taking the time to inquire."

1. *The College Cost Book (1992)*, The College Board Publications, Box 886, New York, NY, 10101-0886. This book contains cost and financial aid information for approximately 3,200 schools in the United States. It details costs of tuition and fees, estimates of books and supplies, and costs of room and board for all types of colleges and universities. It also lists the percentage of students receiving financial aid by grants and scholarships awarded, as well as financial aid deadlines and required forms. For example, the 1992 tuition and fees for Stanford University were $15,102 per academic school year. Books and supplies were estimated at $765, while room and board was $6,159. Nearly half the freshmen were judged to have need-based financial aid requirements, while 60 percent of the freshmen class actually received aid. There are lots of useful financial aid tools, including work sheets that you can use to investigate your ten or so schools in Table 5-2. There is also a very useful bibliography of financial aid sources in the back of *The College Cost Book*. Here's an example:

> *Student Aid Annual, 1991–1992*. Moravia, NY: Chronicle Guidance Publications, 1991. $19.97 plus $2.00 postage and handling. Financial aid programs for students at undergraduate and graduate levels of study, including those offered by noncollege organizations, labor unions, and federal and state governments.

2. *The College Blue Book (Scholarships, Fellowships, Grants and Loans)* (1989), Macmillan Publishing Company, 866 Third Avenue, New York, NY 10022. Specific financial aid information is also discussed in this book. The section on engineering lists fifty-nine agencies and organizations that award scholarships. For example, the Society of Women Engineers (SWE) sponsors approximately thirty-five $1,000–$2,500 scholarships per academic year. Eligibility requirements, application periods, addresses, and phone numbers are all listed. Check it out; that's only one of fifty-nine organizations listed in the engineering section!

3. *The Scholarship Book*, Daniel J. Cassidy and Michael J. Alves, Prentice Hall, Englewood Cliffs, NJ 07632. This book tracks private-sector financial aid opportunities for the student. It claims that more than 65 percent of the scholarships, fellowships, grants, and loans are from the private sector. It also has a bibliography of other funding sources.

Choosing Your School

After you've completed Table 5-2 to the best of your ability, and you've reviewed some of the financial details of each school, start by eliminating the obvious conflicts with your needs. Remember, though, that you're selecting an engineering school *first*, above and beyond many other considerations. Here are examples of obvious conflicts which may cause you to delete a school from the list.

- I'm not a "military" sort of person, and it's absolutely out of the question for me.
- My favorite engineering topic, robotics, is not part of the curriculum.
- My health concerns are such that I need to be near a major hospital in a large city.
- Small private schools are not for me. I really need a broader experience.
- Large schools are not for me. I'm afraid I'll get lost in the shuffle.
- My current family situation requires me to be within a few hours' drive of my hometown.
- The school is not accredited by the engineering board; I won't consider it a viable option.
- The community college credits are not transferable to the university that I want to attend.
- My religious convictions are not represented at this school.
- I'm really concerned about whether or not I'll be accepted to this school, given my grades and/or my ACT or SAT scores.

When you're done with the obvious mismatches and crossed them off the list of schools in Table 5-2, look at the yellow boxes that you've highlighted. Choose the four or so schools (or rows) that have the highest number of boxes highlighted in yellow. If you have a tie between two schools, consider the extra schools as well (i.e., you may have more than four preferred schools). Don't take financial issues into consideration yet—the sky is the limit! Write the names of your preferred schools here.

Preferred Engineering Schools
1.
2.
3.
4.
5.*

*You may have more than four preferred schools if you have "ties" in your scores.

Campus Visits

Once you've identified your preferred engineering schools, arrange a visit to each campus. (Try to visit a few months before the application deadlines.) If you can't afford to make a trip to the school location, beg, borrow, or better yet, save the few hundred dollars so that you can go. Some schools may have special campus visit funds for minority students. Explore this option with the school's admissions office, because a campus visit is a must in your decision-making process.

While on your campus visit, try to set up a tour of key campus locations. If possible, you should speak to professors, guidance counselors, and engineering students and take a look at facilities such as laboratories, the department of the other curriculum that you're seriously considering (athletics, art, dance, economics, religious facilities, etc.), housing (a dorm or a nearby apartment location), the administration office (application process, costs, and other financial information), the financial aid office (talk to a few people about financial aid opportunities), the alumni office (get the names of a few alumni who reside in or near your hometown), the placement office (ask if they have statistics on how many engineering students got jobs in their profession upon graduation from the college last year). If you have enough time, you may want to explore local part-time employment opportunities.

When you sit down to organize your final thoughts, you'll want a record of each school, so be sure to keep a ledger of names, phone numbers, addresses, and notes about your campus visits. Also, shortly after each meeting, summarize your impressions on paper, especially after your discussions with the engineering department. Ask yourself a few questions along the following lines. (Better yet, come prepared to stimulate discussion on these topics—you'll feel more confident about getting the correct impressions of the engineering school.)

1. What are the particulars of getting an engineering degree? What are some of the key requirements? What is the coursework like?
2. Does the school assign engineering guidance counselors for new students? Does it have a mentor program for freshmen?
3. Do you feel that the professors and teaching assistants are readily available for consultation? What is the typical class size? Would you be able to get individualized attention from your professors?
4. Do the laboratory facilities have good equipment? Do they have modern instrumentation and computer equipment?
5. Do you feel welcome in the college of engineering? What are your gut feelings?

Be sure to file all the information that you gathered on your campus visit trips in an orderly fashion. For example, you might group your data in these major categories:

- Engineering Curriculum
- Nonengineering Curriculum
- Administrative and Entrance Requirements
- Finances
- Housing
- Part-Time Employment
- Special Needs

After you've gathered all of this information, let it sit for a while—maybe a few days or so. You're probably approaching the saturation point of useful information right now. If you have too much data and not enough time to assimilate it, things can get confusing in a hurry. Take a small break. You'll need it, especially before school gets started.

Envelope, Please . . . and the Winner Is . . .

Actually, you don't need an envelope. It's not such a mystery; only you can decide who the winner is for you. Let's constructively compare the four or five preferred schools that you've researched to this point. Your campus visit notes will be the main source of information in this final selection process, so get your file out!

First, compare your notes on engineering curriculum. What comments did you write during and after the discussions with the engineering department? Try to organize those comments into two columns of negative and positive statements. Write them below. (For future use you may want to make photocopies of this table of information before you write in it.)

School 1

Pros   Cons

School 2

Pros   Cons

School 3

Pros   Cons

School 4

Pros   Cons

School 5

Pros   Cons

Is there one school that has more substantive negative comments (cons) than the others? Is there any reason to believe that the comments you've listed are not relevant anymore? Think about this list seriously. Remember, if anything changes between now and the time you've been admitted to a school, it's a fairly simple process to update our data using this methodology. You're not "set in concrete" yet! You're still considering your decision, but you've done a lot of constructive research and data assimilation on schools. Feel good about the work you've done to this point!

Getting Accepted to School

After you've reviewed your four or five engineering schools, look at the details of admission for each one. There will be lots of bureaucracy to deal with along the way, including deadlines for school applications and financial aid forms, entrance exam requirements, and personal interviews (perhaps). I'll help you identify the best strategy for your successful entrance to one of your chosen schools.

Marketing Yourself

At first, it may seem a bit odd that marketing would apply to engineering school selection. However, choosing a good engineering school is like choosing a good job. After researching potential employers (or researching potential engineering schools), you've selected several optimum job opportunities (or engineering schools) that suit your needs. The final step in the job-hunting process (or the school-selection process) is getting the job (or getting accepted to the school). You would normally market yourself to your potential employer (or market yourself to your favorite schools) to ensure that you got the job (or ensure that you got accepted into school). Even if you're not exactly the person the employer is looking for (or not the exact student that the school is looking for), you highlight your skills and compatibility with the employer (or highlight your academic and other achievements with the school). By highlighting these skills (or achievements), you have a better chance of getting the job (or getting accepted to the school).

So what's important to highlight in today's admission process? There could be a large number of obvious things such as high GPA, valedictorian of high school class, etc. However, in *Barron's Educational Series*, Harvard dean of admissions Bill Fitzsimmons says: "Most selective universities like strong academic achievement combined with a commitment (not just involvement) in a few extracurricular activities." Although Dean Fitzsimmons emphasizes Harvard's academic excellence entrance requirement, he mentions the importance of a "well-rounded" student too. Not only must a student be involved in extracurricular activities, but the student must make significant contributions to those activities. It's not enough to be involved in a lot of activities without accomplishment of some sort.

Write your marketing strategy here. Include a list of strengths and weaknesses while developing your plan.

My Marketing Strategy

My Strengths

My Weaknesses

My Strategy

Admission Details

You should approach the admissions process as a logical set of necessary details that are part of an organized society. Remind yourself of this thought while you're filling out forms for your schools; otherwise, you might go crazy!

Application Forms. Gather all of the necessary application/admission forms for each school. (Hopefully, you've saved this paperwork from your campus visits.) Here are a few pointers (from the engineering viewpoint) that you should keep in mind while completing the forms.

- Pay attention to detail!
- Be meticulous.
- Complete the forms as accurately and neatly as possible.
- Check and recheck for typographical errors and misspellings. Have someone else check your work.

Since the application form is probably the school's first impression of you, make it a good one. People really pay attention to minute details, and they sometimes develop preconceived notions based on those details. I know that I might be concerned about a future engineer who might design an important object without paying attention to details. Many times, it's the small details that will come back to haunt you!

Here are two details that your application might require.

- Official transcript information including coursework, grades, and class ranking
- Letters of recommendation from past or current teachers, or other distinguished members of the academic community

Admission Requirements. Most schools have a minimum acceptable level of secondary-level educational requirements. You might be required to prove successful completion of English, math, science, and liberal arts coursework by passing an entrance exam, writing an essay, or participating in a personal interview. It is important that you understand exactly what the requirements are for each school and how you can satisfy them.

- *Entrance Exams.* Be aware that different schools may require different exams! Some may require the ACT while others may require the SAT. Some schools will accept either exam score. The basic difference between the two exams is that the SAT rewards a correct answer and penalizes a wrong one. The ACT gives no penalty for wrong answers. There are other format differences too, and the details are found in some of the references already cited. Determine the minimum score requirement for your schools. Also, note that average ACT or SAT scores may vary by school, so find average scores of previous freshmen classes for comparison. This information is found in *Peterson's Four Year Colleges 1995* (see page 57).
- *English Proficiency Exams and Essays.* Many schools require a few paragraphs or a short essay for admission. Some exams suggest a variety of topics to write about, while others ask specific questions, which you are asked to respond to in writing. In either case, market yourself as a human being; speak of your strengths and weaknesses, passions and dislikes, interests and disinterests, goals and ambitions.
- *Personal Interviews.* Most schools don't require a personal interview. However, if your schools have such a requirement, approach this task as though you're interviewing for a job. Accentuate the positive

aspects of your high school education or previous college experiences first, and discuss how you meet or exceed the school's entrance requirements. Emphasize the fact that you're a stellar student (bring some notable item with you to share with the interviewer), and show that you have important accomplishments outside your scholastic life (share some significant experiences in your extracurricular activities).

Be interested and informed. Tell the interviewer that you've done a lot of research on this institution (take the notes you've generated as a result of this book!). Realize that the interview benefits both the school *and* you. Not only does the school learn about your unique accomplishments, but you learn whether or not this is the school for you. Go into the interview with a few questions of your own. Get some answers about the type of educational experience at this school.
- *Financial Aid Forms.* Start working on these as early as possible. Not only is there competition for these resources, but some of your financial aid might be independent of the school you choose. Consider all options!

The Final Decision

After you've done everything that I've suggested, select the school you've been accepted at that best suits your needs. If you're lucky, you'll have several options. Otherwise, the answer may be one school, and that's O.K.; that's the purpose of this exercise. If, however, you've been through this process and none of the schools meet your needs, consider these points.

- Go back to the original four questions and Table 5-2. Are your requirements unusually rigid? Is there more flexibility in some need that you've identified? Make a few modifications in your needs and work through the process again. You must do this quickly since admissions deadlines are near.
- If you can't meet the entrance requirements of the school (e.g., your ACT or SAT scores are not high enough, or you're lacking sufficient secondary coursework), assess the feasibility of provisional or conditional entrance. A school will often accept you based upon your ability to successfully complete a semester or two in college. They may also require you to pass lower-level courses that may not count toward your degree.

▪ 6 ▪

YOU'VE FINALLY ARRIVED AT SCHOOL

This short time period is a milestone in your life! You're about to embark on your journey into the world of engineering school. You may finish school the same person that you are today, or you may not. You may be a wiser person, and then again you may not. You may be an engineer at the end of your school experience, and then again you may not. It's really hard to predict the outcome of your schooling experience, but if you manage it properly, the chances are greater that you'll be an engineering school success story.

Some of my colleagues recalled excitement and fear of the unknown when they started college. Others had a can-do attitude toward the curriculum. Their emotions covered a full spectrum of possibilities. At times, you may be overwhelmed with excitement about the changing future and the possibilities that a new experience will hold for you. Stephanie Witkowski recalls her attitude as she entered the chemical engineering program: "I had that I-can-do-anything feeling and it really gave me the confidence to work hard and do well. I don't remember having any fears about entering engineering school."

John Patterson had a different experience. He came from a small town and went to a large university, and it was a major cultural shock for him. "When you're a big fish in a small pond, it's a lot different than being a small fish in a big pond. I was really concerned that I wouldn't be able to compete with my new peers at the large university that I attended."

How should you deal with your anxieties about college? You may remember President Franklin D. Roosevelt's famous quote while soothing the downtrodden population of the United States during the Depression: "The only thing we have to fear is fear itself." If you research your fears and find some answers, you can make appropriate changes. Consider the engineering curriculum. Your peers might have tried to convince you that this field is impossibly hard. It is going to be challenging, and not everyone will make it. However, if you apply yourself and give it a can-do attitude, you might just find the curriculum enjoyable.

Ingrid Eng doesn't want you to make the same mistake she made. "I came out of high school thinking that I could do anything. This was unfortunate, because I wasn't prepared for the fact that college was very different and more challenging than high school. I definitely should have prepared more and studied harder during my first semester in engineering school. I was assuming that I could study the way I did in high school, and that simply wasn't the case."

To effectively manage your early engineering school experience, consider a few helpful tips from those who have preceded you.

People

Going to engineering school will probably require some major changes in your current relationships; you may be leaving your sense of "people security" behind. You may not see the people that are closest to you on a regular basis. For example, you may not feel that you can confide some of your crazy ideas to some of the new people you're about to meet. However, in order to make this transition process a little easier, you must establish the people connections as soon as you arrive at school. Not only will you feel better about your new environment, but you will have an easier time getting through school if you connect with the right people.

Many new relationships will develop naturally with time, but some you'll need to initiate on your own. These are the key engineering-related relationships that you'll want to cultivate during school.

Engineering Advisor

My colleagues had nearly nonexistent relationships with their advisors, and they regretted that. Pauline Goolsby said, "I remember being given a university catalogue that detailed the exact courses for my engineering degree. I simply checked off the courses as I took them. I had little advice from my advisor concerning options."

Indeed, it is true that nearly all engineering disciplines have rigid course requirements with few options until the junior- and senior-level courses, but a little insight from the advisors about options would have been useful. For example, Steve Doerr took some of his nontechnical classes (history and English) at a local community college and the credits were transferable to his degree at the University of Texas. "It allowed me to really concentrate on my technical coursework," he says.

John Patterson, on the other hand, had a good advisor—strictly by accident. "I nearly missed an appointment with my advisor because I thought he would just rubber-stamp my freshman-year courses. However, during that appointment, he offered me a job in an asphalt research lab at school. Not only did that job supplement my income throughout the remainder of my schooling, but it expanded my knowledge of roadway construction. Ultimately, I got my first job with the Arizona Department of Transportation in part because of my advisor."

John recommends a proactive approach to developing a good rapport with your advisor. When you are assigned an advisor in the school of engineering (obviously, if you're in the EE school, then your advisor should be an EE professor), make an appointment to see this person as soon as possible. Your first meeting should not only be about coursework; it should also be a "fit" test—one in which you'll determine if this advisor is the right one for you. Remember, he or she is there to guide and direct your schooling, and if you have any apprehension about this relationship, then fix it! Request a new advisor if need be.

Mentors

Although your engineering advisor and your mentor could be the same person, you can enhance your engineering experience by finding another person to serve as your mentor. A mentor is usually an experienced engineer or upperclassman who has been through the experiences that you're about to embark upon. This person can serve as your engineering confidant and friend. A mentor can also give you a different perspective than your advisor. First, your mentor can give you individualized attention whereas your advisor may not. Second, your mentor can be a sounding board for serious problems that might arise; you may not want to share all of your doubts and fears with your advisor, and he or she may not have the time to care. This relationship will not develop in a short time period, but you need to cultivate one if at all possible.

Where do you find an engineering mentor? Consider joining an engineering organization first. Steve Doerr said, "I remember being a tutor as an upperclassman, and it seems that this would be a logical place to find a mentor. If you join a professional society in your discipline (e.g., ASCE, AIAA, IEEE), you can start to interact with a few upperclassmen who might be willing to serve as your mentor."

Ingrid Eng recalls that the civil engineering building had a lounge for students to study, talk, and play. It served as a gathering area for all civil engineering students. She says, "I would recommend finding such a gathering spot. It really can serve as as source of synergism among students. You might even find a good mentor in this environment." If such a spot doesn't exist in your school of engineering, then create one!

Friends and Study Groups

Another important aspect to your engineering school experience is to develop a set of friends and form study groups. As it turned out for many of my colleagues and me, our friends were members of our study groups and the members of our study groups were our friends. Study groups not only enhance your engineering school experience; they also serve as a good model of how the real world operates. Ingrid Eng states that "no engineer has ever been able to design, analyze, and construct a structure on his own." It is vital that we engineers work as team members; many of our tasks and projects are simply too complex for any single person to perform.

We all made a similar mistake in our early college years, however. John Patterson says, "I never really started to form study groups until my junior year in school. This was unfortunate, because that sense of synergism simply was not there when I studied alone as a freshman and sophomore." As useful as they are, beware also of wasting time in these groups.

Gregg Skow had a study method that focused people's efforts. Each member of the group would try to study on his or her own for a few days, before the study group convened. "It was much more efficient to work together if we all had done some preliminary studying on our own. It allowed us to solve problems on our own, and get help from others where we needed it."

Steve Doerr and Stephanie Witkowski essentially had no choice in their study groups as freshmen in engineering school. The experience, however, turned into a good one. Steve says, "I was part of a freshman honors program that required a group of twenty engineering students to take all of their classes together. This really forced the issue of forming study groups—one that I think was very beneficial to me." Stephanie's experience was very similar, but her special group was forced to interact on a regular basis with professors too. She says, "This really made the transition process into college much easier. I would recommend a program such as this, but if your school doesn't have one, then make your own study groups as soon as possible!"

Professors and Teaching Assistants (TAs)

Before you register for a course, see if you can't find out who the professor is and do some background research. Dennis Roach said that Georgia Tech University published a book that gave vital statistics on professors' teaching habits. The information summarized the average grades given by a professor for a particular course; the number of hours reserved per week for student/professor consultation; strong teaching points. It also had the professor's response to a series of pertinent questions.

"I remember changing calculus courses in my freshman year," says Dennis. "My first professor was not interested in teaching, and he spoke to the blackboard instead of the students. When I found out about this book, I discovered that he didn't have a very good reputation as a calculus teacher. So I quickly found a professor who made the course fun." Don't be afraid to switch professors—most schools allow this with no penalty during the first few weeks of a course.

If you don't have access to the kind of information Dennis did, you'll naturally develop relationships with professors and TAs very early in your studies anyhow. These relationships will develop for both good and bad reasons. The bad reasons are obvious—you may develop a relationship with a professor because you're doing poorly in a course and you need to seek help. I had a first semester physics course that gave me trouble, and I saw my professor regularly (or, better yet, religiously). Many of my engineering colleagues had troubles with freshman English, and they got to know their TAs quite well. However, don't wait until you're in trouble to get to know your professors!

Early in the semester (or quarter), make an appointment to meet with each professor in his or her office. (Most professors schedule weekly office hours when students can visit.) You can ask questions about goals for the course, and what you're supposed to be getting out of his or her class. As the semester proceeds, get clarification on points that you don't understand during the lecture period. Get help in solving those homework problems that give you trouble. Keep up on these issues and don't wait until the last minute to solve them, because they will more than likely appear on an exam someday.

Pauline Goolsby found another source of help on campus. "I rarely saw my professors and teaching assistants in my freshman and sophomore years. Instead, I took advantage of the tutoring services that the University of Texas at El Paso provided for me. I learned a great deal from an expert in the topic who was not part of my course. Many times, he or she would present the information from a different viewpoint—one that I could understand. Take advantage of these services if they're available at your school!"

Gregg Skow said that his shyness led him to drop his freshman calculus course. "I had a calculus professor who had a very thick foreign accent. It was difficult for me to understand his lectures. Not only that, but I discovered that my background in algebra was not good. I eventually dropped his course because I fell behind, but if I had gone to visit my professor, and worked these problems out, I might not have been so quick to drop the course. I didn't even try to fix the problem! Don't be afraid to approach your professors and TAs when a problem arises." Remember, they're there to give you an education—take advantage of it!

Curriculum

Pauline Goolsby was absolutely correct when she said that the engineering curriculum in your freshman and sophomore years is pretty well set; there will be very few options other than choosing a major discipline to study (e.g., CE, IE, ME, ChemE). In a nutshell, here is a list of generic courses you'll probably take. (Specifics vary by engineering discipline.)

Freshman Year
  Basic Engineering
    Introduction to (EE, CE, ChemE, ME, etc.)
  Math
    Calculus I & II
  Science
    Chemistry I (and perhaps Organic Chemistry) & Labs
    Physics I & Lab
  Other
    English
    Humanities Courses (usually one of the few options available to students—Sociology, Psychology, Humanities, etc.)
    Physical Education (Soccer, Football, Dance, etc.)

Sophomore Year
  Basic Engineering
    Strength of Materials
    Statics
    Dynamics
    Thermodynamics

Math
   Vector Calculus
   Introduction to Ordinary Differential Equations
Science
   Physics II & perhaps more Chemistry
Computer
   Computer Programming Course (C or FORTRAN)

During your freshman year, you'll get a taste of engineering by taking a top-level introductory course in your field of interest. If you have a professor who is a good teacher, this might be an enjoyable experience for you. If, however, you have a professor whose main purpose in life is to scare you away from engineering, don't be afraid. Time after time, in speaking with my colleagues about their introductory course experiences, they characterized it as a "weed out" exercise. Although it was painful to most, they managed to get through the scare tactics unscathed. One colleague even mentioned that the male professor tried to scare the women out of the class by insinuating that they were there to get their Mrs. degree! If such abuse is not for you—do something about it, and talk to some of the people mentioned above! Remember, you're there to learn, and the professors are there to teach!

Of course, the core freshman engineering courses revolve around math and science. If you're uncertain about your skills in math, then don't start with calculus. Make sure that your algebra skills are sufficient before you enter school. John Patterson says, "Because I came from a small town that didn't offer advanced high school math courses, like calculus, I felt that I was at a disadvantage when I got to college." Steve Doerr agrees. "I took calculus as a high school student, and when I took it again in college, I breezed my way through it." Unfortunately, you may be competing with others who had calculus in high school or at a community college, which might put you at a disadvantage. Consider taking this course first at another institution if you develop troubles early on.

Unlike math courses, science courses have labs associated with them. Chemistry and physics always have a lab associated with the normal lectures. These hands-on experiences will help you make reality out of theory, just like the real engineering world. Get the most out of these laboratory experiences and you'll understand the theory much better.

When you're performing your laboratory experiments, you'll usually be part of a team for whatever project that you're working on. However, be sure to be an active part of the team. Help build your experiment; take measurements; assimilate information; draw conclusions. You will understand the point of the experiment much better. In discussing this topic with my female colleagues, a central theme became evident. Insist on doing all of your experimental work and don't let the men take over! Ask questions if you don't understand. There's no such thing as a dumb question.

One female engineer explained the problem like this: Her generation of female engineers helped Mom in the kitchen. The boys helped Dad fix the car and other mechanical devices around the house. This put her at a disadvantage when it came to lab work. She felt that many of the issues that boys "just knew" were not so familiar to her; she took a backseat approach to some of her lab work, because she simply did not have the mechanical hands-on experiences that her brother had. She overcame these frustrations by asking more and more questions and forcing herself to be involved with every part of the experiments.

Another woman said that the men would always second-guess her measurements when she was responsible for recording data for an experiment. "It was a subconscious thing, I'm sure, but it bothered me." If you feel this way, see if you can't speak to your lab partners about this issue. Perhaps they may not realize how they make you feel. Discuss the problem with your study partners, friends, or mentor if need be. There should be no reason for you to feel uncomfortable in the laboratory environment.

Although your basic math and science courses are the foundation for your early engineering education, English deserves special mention, because some engineers struggle with this subject. Remember that good communication skills are important in all aspects of your career. If you have an excellent technical idea, but you struggle to communicate it well, you may lose out. So take good English courses to polish your written skills and take an oral communications course to sharpen your verbal skills.

If you are struggling with English, you may want to consider John Patterson's experience. He took an English course that specialized in German literature. He says, "Not only was I not interested in this topic, but if I got a C or lower in this course I would be put on probation with my scholarship. As a result of this experience, I felt like I didn't have the right stuff to get through college. It was really demoralizing." He eventually dropped this particular English course to avoid getting a C. "At the time, I thought that dropping a course was the end of the world, but I got through this by taking an English course at a community college." He simply transferred his English credit to the University of Arizona, and avoided the whole problem. John's advice is that you shouldn't be afraid to drop a course if you're getting a bad grade—you'll make it up somehow.

Activities Unrelated to Coursework

Your coursework at times will seem extremely hard and burdensome. To relieve your stress and mental fatigue, you need a "pressure relief valve." This can be in the form of exercising, playing a sport, going to a movie, reading a good novel, or volunteering your time to some worthy cause.

All of my colleagues recommended some form of outside activity that not only keeps you sane but also makes you a well-rounded person. These outside experiences will give you a sense of balance in your life; it's so easy to wrap yourself in the engineering school world and lose your proper perspective on life. Stephanie Witkowski remembers studying most of the time, but she always attended the school football games. Steve Doerr played rugby. After many long hours of studying, Ingrid Eng spent a few moments bantering with friends over dessert. John Patterson went to happy hour on a regular basis. Everybody needs these outside experiences.

Other Options

Not everybody will be like Tommy Goolsby. From the day Tommy was born, he was making something, playing with his tools, and helping his dad in the construction business. Tommy actively participated in science projects as far back as he could remember. He started his college years in mechanical engineering and finished his master's degree in mechanical engineering without any gyrations or aberrations in his schedule.

Most of us had doubts about engineering school that caused us to take a less linear school path. This circuitous route can take various forms:

1. Student who started in another field—then entered and completed engineering school.
2. Student who started in engineering school—left—but eventually reentered and completed engineering school.
3. Student who started in another field—then entered engineering school—but eventually left.
4. Student who started in engineering school—then left.

Mary Young started her career as a social worker, then turned machinist, then turned mechanical engineer. She says, "It took me quite a number of years sorting through various options before I settled on mechanical engineering." Gregg Skow is an example of the second category. "I picked mechanical engineering simply because I had to pick something. I became disinterested, so I transferred to a business college. I took courses toward an accounting degree, but the challenge and satisfaction weren't there. I eventually went to the systems engineering college and graduated in that field. These changes only cost me a year's time in school, although at the time it seemed like an eternity."

Pauline Goolsby started her college career in accounting. She became disinterested and gradually began taking engineering courses in her sophomore year, although she had not officially transferred to the engineering college. She graduated with a degree in industrial engineering, but later went back to school to get her teaching certificate. She teaches high school math now and enjoys it tremendously.

Dawn Cowan started her college years at the University of Texas in petroleum engineering. "During the early 1980s when the oil industry was booming, I thought I wanted a fast-paced career where all the action was. Unfortunately, this curriculum was not for me." She explored many different avenues, and accidentally took an archaeology course that really intrigued her. She eventually graduated with a general studies degree, specializing in anthropology, French, and history. "Approximately ten years later, I now know that I did the right thing," says Dawn. "I would recommend to all engineering students that they take a few fun classes that are completely unrelated to engineering. You might discover, as I did, a more appropriate field of study."

Horror Stories

Imagine this scenario. There you are, sitting in your freshman chemistry course, struggling through your first exam. Suddenly, the professor says, "Time is up. Pass your exam papers to me." You've suddenly realized that you didn't complete the exam. You were methodically working your way through the questions, and you simply did not finish. Anxiety sets in. You go home, and think that your college career is over—you just know that you failed that exam because you didn't complete each question. This happened to Jon Rogers during his freshman year at Iowa State University. He says, "It was very frustrating for me to get used to the fact that many of my exams were designed for incompletion. I used to complete all of my exams in high school, but in college it wasn't the same."

There will be moments in your early school years that create a lot of anxiety, frustration, and doubt. How do people deal with these tense moments? How can you learn from the mistakes of others? Let me share a few with you, and we can draw some conclusions.

Dennis Roach was taking his last exam for the winter quarter in his jet propulsion course. He knew that his grade was a borderline B/C going into the exam. As he worked his way through the exam, he didn't understand many of the problems or how to approach them. He knew he was floundering, and he started to hyperventilate. Dennis says, "I felt like I was the only one who didn't understand many of the questions. As it turned out, most of the other students didn't understand the questions either. I worried for nothing. I eventually survived the course, and I don't think that hyperventilating was worth it."

Many college professors grade on the curve. This means that the professor calculates an average score of all students, and a Gaussian distribution (also called the bell curve) is used to set break points for grades. Simply put, the large majority of students receive C's, while a small fraction of students receive A's and F's. Nearly all of my colleagues and I remember receiving grades of 30, 40, and 50 percent on exams, which translated into A's, B's, and C's in most instances. Thank God for the grading on a curve, because we all would have flunked out of school without it.

Pauline Goolsby has some good advice for dealing with this issue. She says, "Remember that no one is meant to get all of the answers. Always be sure to check your method and the steps you've taken to get an answer. Oftentimes, professors are more concerned with your thought process than the bottom-line answer. You'll usually get partial credit if your methodology was sound even if your answer was wrong."

Although Pauline's advice generally holds true, I had an experience with a physics course in which partial credit was not in the professor's vocabulary. My professor announced that he wanted to teach his students a lesson about getting the right answer. He designed his exams with ten relatively simple problems to work out in fifty minutes. The catch was that once these problems were solved, you simply circled one of seven possible answers. (You'll find that multiple-choice physics exams are very difficult!) The professor knew exactly where you might go astray in solving these problems, and so even if my answer resembled one of the seven choices, it wasn't always the correct one.

The professor and I had many long discussions about his philosophy of grading. I felt that it was unfair that he did not consider my thought process in grading my exams. It was demoralizing to get 40 percent on an exam, even though it translated to a B grade. He said that he gave no partial credit on exams because he worked in industry for ten years where in many situations the wrong answer could endanger the general public and getting the right answer was crucial. Needless to say, I learned a good lesson from him and I certainly understand his viewpoint, but I still believe that the learning environment should not be so cut-and-dried.

The real value of that experience for me was learning that I was scared to death of my professors for no good reason. When I charged into my professor's office, ready to disagree with him about his grading philosophy, he said to me, "Your problem is not with my grading system. Your problem is with physics. Let's schedule a time period so that I can help you with physics." And so I spent one hour per week with my professor, being tutored on the nuances of physics. I was lucky, because I saw him early enough in the semester to work things out. Don't delay seeing your professor if you find yourself in trouble!

The Mother of All Horror Stories

John Patterson was granted a very good academic scholarship to attend engineering school. One requirement was that he maintain a 3.5 of 4.0 grade point average (GPA). John says, "Talk about stress! I really had no cushion to fall back on (that is, little or no family financial support). I thought that if I didn't maintain my GPA, I'd lose my scholarship and my opportunity in engineering school."

In his second semester of his freshman year, John had 16 or 17 units of classes and he worked long hours at the asphalt lab for his professor. Going into his final exams, he had A's and B's in all of his classes. Unfortunately, he blew all of his finals, and he ended up with B's and C's. In short, he didn't have a 3.5 average for the semester.

"I remember going home after I checked all of my final grades. I lay on the couch for what seemed like an eternity, agonizing over my major screw-up. I really thought that I would simply leave college, never to attend again." Fortunately, said John, he was able to swap his 3.5 scholarship for a less stringent 3.0 scholarship. As soon as the pressure was off, he bounced right back the next semester with a 3.6 GPA.

John says, "I was able to relax more when the pressure was off, and I learned more from my courses. I also learned to tell when I should drop a class before disaster struck. Don't be afraid to drop a class if things aren't working out!"

The Most from Your Early Years

In this chapter, I've tried to give you a heads-up on how to deal with your freshman and sophomore years. It doesn't have to be painful. There will, however, be a few tense moments, but you should have a better idea of what to expect and how to handle these situations. Get the most from your early years, because you may spend a lifetime dealing with these experiences as a professional. Not only that, but you may meet a lifetime friend or a spouse or get a job as a result of these experiences.

· 7 ·

WORKING PART-TIME

The bills are piling up. There's tuition, books, laboratory fees, school supplies. Your scholarship, grant, or loan doesn't cover everything. What about rent and transportation? Oh, and by the way, don't forget that you're supposed to eat too! Hey, maybe you want to see a movie or a play sometime.

Things just aren't adding up dollarwise. You're midway through your sophomore year and you fear that the bill collector is going to haul you off to jail. Nobody would give you a credit card because yours are spent to the limit already. More worries!

Don't get yourself in a financial bind. It will affect your studies, your health, and your state of mind. Engineering school is tough enough without worrying where your next meal is coming from. You need a pressure relief valve—one that gets you away from the campus environment. When you get away from campus, consider doing something constructive with your time. How about a part-time job?

You're probably thinking that this is impossible in view of your already overloaded school schedule. What about the weekly lab report that takes the better part of several evenings to complete? What about the lengthy readings and homework that you must do daily to keep from falling behind?

You're busy in engineering school, but students have survived engineering school and part-time work. It can be a valuable and rewarding experience from both a technical and a financial viewpoint. Not all knowledge is gained from books, and a little on-the-job training can be very educational. Also, working can open doors for you in the technical community. Some students who had technically oriented jobs learned that engineering wasn't for them, which saved time and money. In learning these things, you might find that you can pay your bills too.

The Dollar Experience

You may end up with a survival job. Even though you've scanned the ads, called everyone you knew, and worked through the school placement office, you may not get a job in your field of interest. Good summer jobs get filled quickly. Good school-year jobs may not match your school schedule requirements. And so you took what you could get. However, that doesn't mean that you won't learn or gain anything from your work experiences.

Although I lived at home, and my parents provided free room and board as long as I maintained my grades, I took two part-time jobs during my college years. The first was as a busboy in a local ice-cream store and restaurant. This job enabled me to purchase a car, pay for insurance, and buy gasoline. There was very little money left over for social activities. However, the experience was not useless. I learned how to manage money in the real world. I learned that running a small business requires a lot of time for the owner. I learned that I must be responsible in my work, no matter what it is.

My second work experience was more substantive than the first. I worked as a lab technician for a metal-plating shop not far from the university, which allowed me to work in a scientific field. I analyzed metal-plating solutions for chemical content using standard laboratory techniques such as titration and pH measurement. Once I determined the chemical content of a solution, I adjusted the plating bath so that the process would produce the desired results.

I studied the chemical issues that created problems in the large baths, and developed a process to troubleshoot the anodizing and plating operations. I performed many experiments to determine the optimum way to keep the processes running, and I learned that working in the chemical field was not for me, even though my grandfather was a research chemist.

I also learned that it was next to impossible to work a job that didn't allow flexible hours. My boss understood that I was a student first and that I must successfully complete my education. He allowed me to work around my classroom hours and my exam schedules. This is a requirement that you must make clear to your boss at the very beginning.

CO-OP Experience

CO-OP (Cooperative) student programs vary from university to university, but generally they provide an organized plan for the student's entire college career that allows for alternating semesters of school and work. Typically, this adds to your time in school.

Dennis Roach participated in such a program when he went to Georgia Tech for his bachelor's degree. The mechanical engineering department allowed him to attend school for three quarters and work for two quarters. The work was engineering-related and he earned good money.

His first job experience came very early in his studies—the summer between his freshman and sophomore years. He worked in Jacksonville, Florida, for the Naval Air Rework Facility. "Even at this early stage in my engineering studies, my employer allowed me to study and work on P-3, A-6, and A-7 aircraft." The job involved surveying aircraft for fatigue; analyzing structures and systems; and performing reverse engineering of crashes. "Many times we would take the insides of the aircraft out, such as the landing gears or the instrumentation system, and engineer new systems. It was very satisfying work, especially for a student studying aerospace engineering." Interestingly enough, his current research involves the study of aging aircraft. "Who would have thought that I would be doing something related to my first engineering job as a full-time career!"

Although Dennis's plan was to stick with the CO-OP program throughout his bachelor's studies, he left the program after his stint with the Naval Air Rework Facility. "Although it was an enjoyable experience, the CO-OP program wanted me to go back to Jacksonville. However, I wanted to try another field."

For his next work experience, he scanned professional publications, wrote letters, and sent résumés to companies that were advertising in the American Institute of Aerospace and Aeronautical (AIAA) engineers' magazine, and other publications such as *Aviation Week*. "I was amazed at the response. I ended up with four job offers to choose from!" Although he was not in the university's CO-OP program anymore, the school gave him permission to work for four quarters at whichever job he chose. He went to work for McDonnell Douglas in Houston.

It was an exciting time to work as a subcontractor for NASA in Houston. The first space shuttle flight was due to go up in the summer of 1981. "I knew that this moment in time was truly a milestone, and I wanted to be part of it." Dennis took an aggressive approach in requesting interesting and challenging engineering projects to support the first shuttle mission. "I worked to create a model of the trunnions for the development flight instrumentation payload. I also helped analyze stresses in the skin of the space shuttle as it reentered the earth's atmosphere. I even programmed astronaut Neil Young's personal handheld calculator as a backup to onboard systems. The fact that Young was a Georgia Tech alumnus made it all that much more exciting for me."

Dennis's CO-OP experiences were invaluable to his education as well as his professional knowledge of engineering. "I would highly recommend that you take advantage of such work experiences, because they make your studies more realistic and easier to understand. Not only that, but you'll discover precisely what you are or aren't interested in."

Unfortunately, not all CO-OP experiences are as rewarding as Dennis's. Pauline Goolsby went to the placement office at the University of Texas at El Paso to find an engineering-related job. It was her senior year, and she was finally overcoming a physical ailment that sapped much of her energy during her early school years. "I had several jobs lined up, complete with job offers, but when I went for my physicals, they rejected me. I didn't need the stress at the time, so I dropped the issue. Finally, however, I got a job in a manufacturing plant that made harnesses for wiring under cars."

The job allowed her to take courses in the morning and work in the afternoons. "Although this company worked in my field of interest (industrial engineering), my job was in a quality control department that didn't give me any challenging engineering assignments." Pauline admits that she could have been more aggressive in requesting challenging tasks. "It seemed as though the guys who were in the same program as I were given the fun engineering projects while I was given the office work." As a result she didn't accomplish what she set out to do. "I wanted to work in industrial engineering and make a few job connections prior to my graduation. However, I didn't learn anything about industrial engineering and I didn't make any job connections." Ultimately, Pauline's decision to go back to school to become a math teacher grew out of this experience.

The Part-Time Work Experience

All of my colleagues had part-time work experiences in college. During their freshman and sophomore years, their experiences were much like mine—working as a busboy, waiter, waitress, plumber's assistant, and driving a van. A few had technically oriented jobs such as a machinist, a research assistant, and a teaching assistant.

The Machinist

Mary Young had a psychology degree from a community college in Missouri, and she was working as a social worker, but she knew that she wanted to do something with her hands. So she entered a machinist's school and spent a year studying the trade.

"After graduating, I worked as a machinist in a local shop. I enjoyed my job and I was making good money, but I knew I could do more. I soon found my aptitude for machine design as a result of this experience." Mary discovered that the University of Arkansas was looking for a machinist to support their research activities. "Four people applied for the job. We were all given the same project, a laser mirror mount, to complete. I won the competition and got the job." Although she was ecstatic about her new opportunity, she took a tremendous cut in pay at this job. "The money wasn't important, though, but the chance to go to school was."

After she began work, she discussed her interest in continuing her education with the director of research services. "As a university employee, I was allowed to take one class per semester. My forty-hour-per-week job came first, though." Fortunately, as a result of her previous coursework, she started mechanical engineering school at the sophomore level. "I took my coursework at night whenever I could, but the university let me work flexible hours if I had to take courses during the day."

It took Mary six years to complete her degree. "It was a good thing that the director of research services supported me in my endeavor. I'm not sure that this would have been possible without the flexibility he gave me so that I could work around my course schedule. I was very lucky to have such an opportunity." Perhaps, like Mary Young, you have another skill or talent that you can capitalize on. Be aggressive and don't be afraid to open the door when opportunity knocks.

The Professor's Research Assistant

Jon Rogers began looking for part-time work during his sophomore year at Iowa State University. He got to know one of his professors who needed an assistant to run experiments. "My professor had a research grant that allowed him to study fluid flow problems through corrugated fuel lines in supersonic transport vehicles." During the late 1970s, the Concorde supersonic jet was popular. "I simply asked him if he had enough funding to hire me for ten hours per week. He said yes, and I had a job." The work supported Jon throughout his sophomore year until the funding dried up.

Fortunately, another research grant came in, and the professor asked Jon to continue as his assistant. "The project was studying sound environments at Air Force bases. I was interested in acoustics, and it was very intriguing to me." Jon produced sound contour plots that were ultimately used to increase the environmental database on noise at airfields. "The funding dried up on this project too, but it was a great way to work in a real research environment while I attended school."

The Professor's Teaching Assistant

Keri Sobolik doesn't remember exactly how she got her sophomore-year job. "I think I must have talked to the department head at the University of New Mexico," she says. It wasn't the most glamorous job. "I simply graded papers for a professor who taught dynamics." It paid money, though, and she learned something from her experience.

"Since I had already been through this course, I was familiar with the content. However, when you grade papers, you begin to understand where students go wrong. In this way, you can learn a lot about the topic. I really became very comfortable with the concepts in dynamics as a result."

Although Keri never taught this particular course, she discovered something about teaching techniques. "I thought that the professor should have an idea where students were having problems. Since I rarely had interactions with the dynamics professor, I felt that he didn't know which concepts the students weren't grasping. When I got into graduate school and taught courses myself, I remembered this experience and I tried not to fall into the same trap." Keri's experience of grading papers is much like being a tutor. You learn a lot by teaching a course (or grading papers) yourself!

The Summer Work Experience

Most engineering students take summer jobs in their field, which benefits both students and companies. The student can concentrate on real-world activities without being distracted by coursework, and the company can survey the bright young minds that are soon to graduate from school. Regard it as an opportunity to fine-tune your interests in engineering school, while earning money.

The Nuclear Power Plant

As a young nuclear engineering student, Samantha Lapin had an opportunity that many would envy. "Through the placement office at school, I was hired for two consecutive summers to work at the Palo Verde Nuclear Power Plant in Arizona. It was an opportune moment for me as a nuclear engineer. The plant was in the construction phase, and I was a part of it." Her first summer's experience was one of total observation. "I was essentially a gofer, but I was in the environment to watch the reactor get put together." During her second summer, however, she worked on an engineering assignment, and actually made some calculations. "I did my work in radiation monitoring, and I had a mentor who took me under his wing. It was a great working relationship."

Even though her experiences were positive, she learned that she didn't want to work at a nuclear power plant after she graduated from school. "I realized that I was interested in plant design, not operations. I would have to design new plants or work in another nuclear engineering specialty." Since the United States has not built very many nuclear power plants since Palo Verde, Sam chose another field—systems analysis of space nuclear propulsion systems.

The On-the-Road Experience

John Patterson really needed a job for the summer; his funds were running short and he was concerned about meeting his obligations the next school year. He had a part-time job during the school year, but that was just enough for him to get by. Summer could be an opportunity to get ahead, but only with a good job.

John applied for a summer job through the placement office at school. Because there were few technically oriented jobs and too many engineering students, he didn't think he'd find anything. He was particularly interested in getting a job with the Arizona Department of Transportation (ADOT) because it was near his hometown.

A few days after he arrived home, he got word that ADOT wanted him for the summer. "I was really surprised, because I never had an interview or personal contact with this agency. My only interaction with them was my job application, which was sent in by mail. I was lucky."

The job was quite varied. He worked on several highway construction projects in remote areas of southern Arizona. He worked on a survey crew; he painted stripes on highways; and he repaired and reconstructed highway bridges. As a young civil engineering student whose interest was roadway construction, he was happy to have the job. "Although my tasks were somewhat trivial at times, I learned that new construction of *anything* was exciting to me; being in that environment was fun. Ultimately, I chose to work in this field as a result of this early experience."

The Computer Experience

Steve Sobolik knew that he wanted to be near his family during his summer breaks from school. While he was on spring break (sophomore year) from Texas A&M University, he visited his parents in Houston and he decided to get serious about a summer job. "For that whole week, I sent my résumé to a number of technical companies in Houston—NASA and TRW, to name a few. It was my first experience in applying for a technical summer job, and I discovered that many of the summer positions available for engineering students were taken by the spring break. I should have done this during the Christmas break."

When summer came and Steve returned home to Houston, he was disappointed that he didn't have a job. "I was resigned to the fact that I would drive a van as I did the previous summer." After a few days at home, he got a phone call from a firm named Mitre. They offered him a summer job as a computer programmer.

Although Steve was studying mechanical engineering, he felt that this was an opportunity that he didn't want to pass up. Since Mitre was a contractor to NASA and the Johnson Space Center in Houston and the space shuttle program was going strong (circa 1980), he worked on the mission control mainframe computer project, which involved the updating of a 1969 computer system. He wrote computer codes with other computer scientists to support the new machine that was soon to be brought on-line.

"As a result of my computer programming experiences that summer, I developed an interest in applying mechanical engineering problem solving to computers. I also enjoyed the work enough so that I returned to Mitre the following summer and continued the project."

Do-It-Yourself Summer Jobs

Steve Doerr wasn't going to wait for anyone to do him a favor. He called or wrote lots of companies for his summer jobs, and he did all of the legwork himself. "I continually scanned newspapers, professional/technical publications, and talked to professors." He landed his first job after his freshman year in aerospace engineering. Steve was lucky to get a worthwhile summer technical job so early.

"I knew people who worked at the Applied Research Lab that was connected to the University of Texas. I just kept bugging them until they gave me a job." Although his main assignment was soldering and wiring sonar boxes, he got involved in a sunspot project. He plotted sunspot data and asked questions about the inferences from his plots. It was his first experience at scientific research.

To find his next summer job, he made phone calls and sent résumés out early in the fall. As a result, he hired on with Boeing in Seattle. "Although it was a drafting job for wind tunnel model support, it was related to my aerospace engineering interests." Working for an aerospace company was fun, but he learned that drafting was not for him.

He continued his quest for varied experiences, and one of his professors helped him land his next job, with Southwest Research Institute in San Antonio, Texas. "It was another good experience, programming computers, interpreting data, and working odd jobs around the office."

Other Useful Work Experiences

People find jobs in all sorts of ways. Some people are in the right place at the right time; some people know the right people; some people read bulletin boards.

The Cement Connection

"I was all set to work for Lawrence Livermore National Laboratory (L^3) one summer," said Ingrid Eng. However, much to her disappointment, the program she was to work on was canceled.

Although it was a little late to apply for summer jobs, she quickly called on an engineering contact she had recently met. Ingrid says, "I had written a paper for my technical writing course about Portland Cement, and I had gotten a company representative to provide detailed technical information. I also knew him from my participation in the American Society of Civil Engineers. I called him, explained my jobless dilemma, and told him I would volunteer for the summer. I just wanted work experience related to civil engineering—paid or not!"

Although the company representative did not have a paid engineering intern job for the summer at Portland Cement, he knew that the county had such a program, and recommended Ingrid for it. He made a phone call or two, and before she knew it she had an interview.

"After my interview and successful completion of a test, I got the job!" says Ingrid. She started out with drafting odds and ends and carrying out a few minor engineering assignments. Her boss was knowledgeable enough to give her just enough information to find her own solutions to problems. "It was a great working environment, because I worked with a group of experienced engineers who took an interest in showing me the ropes." As a result of her excellent performance during this summer, she was asked to stay as a part-time employee during her senior year of school.

"My work became more challenging and interesting. I got involved in proposals, contracts, and specifications. During this period, the Tucson area had hundred-year flooding (in technical terms, this means a severe flood that happens only once in a hundred years) which presented the county with many new civil engineering design challenges. It was an exciting time to work for the county." Although she readily admits that it was tough going to school and working part-time, she says the county tried to accommodate her school schedule and interests. "It's hard, but keep your chin up," says Ingrid. "I got an offer for a full-time job after graduation. You never know how your school-related work experiences are going to turn out, but you won't know until you try!"

The Tour Guide

Keri Sobolik's future brother-in-law dated an engineer's daughter. That's how she got her chance to work in the research and development (R&D) environment she had always dreamed of. "I found out about an R&D job through a convoluted series of contacts, and I worked part-time through my junior year in college as a solar technology transfer specialist at Sandia National Laboratories." Although her title sounded impressive, Keri said that she really acted as a tour guide for the solar energy department at Sandia.

"It was the post-Jimmy Carter years, and dollars were unfortunately scarce for the solar energy programs. I got to interact with many renowned scientists across the country, but my job fizzled as the dollars decreased. As a result of this experience, however, I learned that I wanted to work in the research and development environment. I also discovered that if I worked in this environment, my credibility would be enhanced if I had a master's degree in engineering."

Hardening of the Arteries and the Bulletin Board

When Dennis Roach wasn't working as a CO-OP student, he concentrated on school. However, he sought the most valuable engineering work experiences that he could. And so he had a light school schedule one quarter that involved only twelve hours of courses. He went to his mechanical engineering professors and asked them if he could do technical research on a volunteer basis.

He discovered that one professor had interesting (though unpaid) work related to fluid dynamics. "Although I was directed to perform some fairly routine tasks, I studied the relationship between fluid flow and hardening of the arteries. I set up and performed experiments at the direction of my professor. I would recommend such hands-on experience to any engineering student."

During his senior year in school, Dennis scanned the bulletin boards around campus for a job, and he discovered a program that caught his eye: International Exchange of Students for Technical Experience. On a whim, he applied for a job. Much to his surprise, he was accepted as a research fellow with the National Aerospace Laboratory in Holland. He spent a summer working on stress analysis problems related to critical joints in structures. Dennis says, "Not only was it a worthwhile technical experience, but I learned a lot about another country and its culture."

What This Means to Me

From tour guides to lab technicians; from machinists to computer programmers; from draftsperson to research fellow. All of the part-time experiences were worthwhile. Some are bound to be more valuable than others, but as a whole, it's an experience that you need to consider.

It will expand your knowledge of the engineering profession as no textbook can; it will open up doors to the future that would have otherwise remained closed. It will bring in a few bucks that could see you through the lean college years.

Keri Sobolik says that she didn't have to work for money during school. She was able to live at home and concentrate on her studies, but she still recommends the work experience. It's a good way to find out if you'll even like working in the engineering profession. "It's better to learn this early before you waste a lot of time in engineering school," says Keri.

The other lessons learned from these experiences are far less dramatic, but are important. You should learn that engineers must perform tasks accurately and precisely; engineers must ask questions and not take things at face value; and engineers must show enthusiasm and get involved. Ingrid Eng says, "Get the experience whether it pays or not. It could be invaluable!"

Sometimes you have to be in the right place at the right time. However, if you maximize your exposure to the right groups of people, your chances improve. Don't forget to consider the following resources in your quest for a job.

CO-OP Opportunities
University Placement Offices
Professors
Professional Points of Contact
Family and Friends
Want Ads in Professional Publications
Local Businesses
Nationwide Businesses
Professional/Technical Organizations
School Bulletin Boards

Remember that you must be proactive—it isn't going to happen unless you make it happen. Be aggressive. Start looking for that summer job in the fall. Write letters; make phone calls; send résumés; follow up. You'll be amazed at the responses you get if you just work the job scene.

• 8 •

BEING AN UPPERCLASSMAN

You've just been through the worst of it. Introduction to Engineering 101 is over; statics and dynamics are over; physics and ordinary differential equations are history. It's time to get more serious about your specific field of interest. What do you really want to study in your last two years of school?

If you're an electrical engineering student, you must now choose among a host of specialties—communications, neural networks, and circuit design, to name a few. If you're a mechanical engineering student, you must choose among machine design, robotics, and others. If you're a civil engineering student, you must decide among structural, transportation, geotechnical, and others. Lots of choices; lots of decisions yet to come.

The selection of a specialty is probably the most important decision of your final years in undergraduate school. But how do you go about making that decision?

Your Engineering History

Believe it or not, you now have some engineering experiences of your own that you can draw upon! Think back to your first few years of engineering school, and see if you can't discover a few clues about the engineering specialty you should select as an upperclassman.

A. List three courses that you did best in during your freshman and sophomore years.

1.

2.

3.

B. List three courses that you enjoyed the most. (Be honest with yourself here.)

1.

2.

3.

C. What professors or teaching assistants did you develop a rapport with? (If you have taken the proactive learning approach by getting to know your professors or teaching assistants, this should be an obvious answer. However, if you just enjoyed their style of teaching and never consulted them during office hours, that's O.K. too.)

1.

2.

3.

D. List the work experiences that you've had in the last two years.

1.

2.

3.

E. List the types of reading materials you've enjoyed over the last two years. (The answer to this question doesn't have to be technical journals or publications. It could mean that you've discovered an interest in a few new magazines, such as *Scientific American, Aviation Week, Popular Science,* or *Popular Mechanics.*)

1.

2.

3.

After you've answered these questions, analyze your answers. If your favorite course was EE 101, if your favorite teaching assistant was an EE graduate student, if your favorite job was working with an electronics gadget firm, and if your favorite reading material was the electronic gadgetry catalogue, then you may want to consider an engineering specialty in manufacturing of electrical components.

Perhaps this simplified approach to determining your specialty is not revealing any useful answers. If that's the case, then consider other engineering stories.

The Experienced Engineer's Story on Selection of Engineering Specialties

All of the engineers who discussed the engineering specialty selection process gave different answers. Some remembered very few elective choices as upperclassmen; some made arbitrary selections. So what about the logical "scientific method" that I promoted?

"I had only three technical electives available to me during my undergraduate years at UTEP," says Tommy Goolsby. "That was good for me, though." UTEP is a hands-on school that provides lots of experiments and lab work. "It's not a deeply theoretical environment, and I went there because of the focus on experimental work. The school did not have a lot of choices because of its small size, but it suited my needs quite well.'

Stephanie Witkowski said, "I chose to take more electives in business-related fields and other areas rather than the engineering field. I knew that I would have the advanced chemical engineering coursework that all of my peers had, but I wanted to broaden myself a little." Stephanie took some management and marketing courses as well as political science and environmental classes to support and enhance her interest in chemical engineering. In the end, Stephanie was probably more marketable than some of her peers, because of her choice of nontechnical electives.

Not all engineering students have the same experiences as upperclassmen. Many make opportunities available to themselves. If you march onward through your engineering school without studying your options, then you must be as sure of your interest as Tommy Goolsby was. However, if you're like many others, you may want to explore different specialties.

How do you go about doing this? Some engineers based their decisions on the courses or experiences of their freshman and sophomore years. Steve Doerr said that doing exceptionally well in his dynamics course spurred his interest in aerodynamics. "Although the course was tough and very challenging, I had a good professor who made things clear to me. I took this into account when I finally decided to study aerodynamics rather than some other field in aerospace engineering."

A good work experience might also influence your decision. Steve Wilson chose transportation engineering over many other possibilities because of his work in the construction field. He spent time as a laborer in an asphalt-manufacturing plant where he became aware of the need for research in materials. "I finally got a job at the university researching recycled asphalt and concrete processes. Between this and my experiences as a laborer, I realized that I had developed a niche for myself."

He spent nearly six years working in the industry and going to school for his bachelor's degree in civil engineering. While most of us hurried our way through school, anxious to enter the real world at the ripe old age of twenty-one or twenty-two, we probably could have benefited from Steve's approach to the engineering specialty selection process. He took his time to figure out what he wanted to do, which finally paid off. "Don't feel obligated to stick to your curriculum," says Dawn Cowan. "If you don't get out in four years, it's not the end of the world. Have some fun! Take advantage of the university learning environment while it's available to you. Take a foreign language or some other course that sounds intriguing."

Senior Project Courses

One of the more gratifying experiences as an engineer is to make theory a reality. After all of the coursework—math, science, and lab experiments—the senior engineering student is usually required to produce a project. This activity demonstrates your knowledge of the engineering trade; your application of engineering principles to real-world problems; and your ability to get the job done. Usually, it results in a report, an experiment, or a piece of hardware or software.

Sometimes seniors are required to take a three-credit project course, while others are not. Many students may have projects through other coursework, engineering societies, or work experiences. Whatever the experience will be for you, an engineering project is something to look forward to. Don't fall into this trap:

I dreaded my senior project course because:

- I didn't have an interesting project.
- My professor didn't seem interested in guiding me.

- My enthusiasm was waning at this particular point in my schooling. (I was quickly approaching burnout.)

Remember the following points while doing your senior project.

1. Do something that interests you.

If you're a hands-on sort of person, then get a hands-on project. If you're a theoretical sort of person, then do some research and analysis; write a paper or a report. If you're a hardware sort of person, design some hardware. If you're a software sort of person, develop some software. Or perhaps you're interested in analysis and software development and you could combine the two into a single project. These statements might sound very simplistic, but you'd be amazed at the things that you might forget about yourself as you embark on your senior project.

Tommy Goolsby was a hands-on problem solver who liked to implement mechanical designs. One requirement of his senior mechanical design course was to complete a project with other team members, which involved the printing of envelopes on large printers for IBM. He and his design team developed an attachment to feed the envelopes into the printer. "It was a real-world problem that interested me. We were able to develop a solution for the customer." In short, this project had clearly defined objectives and goals that allowed the team to design and implement a satisfactory solution.

2. Find a professor, advisor, or sponsor who supports and guides your project.

Your project will be more meaningful to you if you have a customer who is interested in your results. This customer should be an experienced engineer such as a professor, your advisor, or a sponsor in private industry. In some cases, however, you may not have to develop your customer. Some engineering departments have established ties with private industry. For example, Tommy Goolsby's senior project was assigned to him because UTEP had connections with the local business leaders at IBM. IBM needed help, and the senior project course was a useful resource for them. In another case, Walt Witkowski knew a chemical engineering professor who needed help translating a computer program from a PC format to an Apple format. He took on the task as a senior project.

In many cases, however, you must find your own project. In some cases this can be good, because you can do what you want. In other cases it can be bad, because you may not find one that suits you.

You might find an interesting project by talking to your professors, advisor, or employer about their needs for your engineering services. After all, these services are essentially free to the customer, and they'll want to take advantage of this opportunity for that reason alone! Steve Wilson was able to develop a materials project from his connections with the asphalt business. "At the direction of my employer, I was already setting up experiments to determine asphalt material properties. I expanded the scope of my job to determine the best test method for different shapes and sizes of asphalt specimens. I was able to perform an interesting senior project while my employer, the civil engineering department, benefited from my research."

3. Allow enough time in your schedule to successfully complete your project.

Project courses are always time-consuming. The answers aren't conveniently located in the back of a textbook; no project is exactly like another. Also, there are many elements of a project that are truly time-consuming that aren't necessarily technical. Who is going to gather your equipment for your experiment? In most cases you'll have to scrounge around. Who is going to fix your equipment when it breaks? You can't afford to pay someone on your tight, practically nonexistent budget. Who is going to take the data a second time because the first set was bad? Who is going to reduce the data for the second time because you discovered a bug in your computer routine?

Get control of your time and plan your senior project. Rather than jumping into the middle of a project, see if you can't identify major milestones first. Then set up a time schedule to meet those milestones. The project plan doesn't have to be elaborate; it may be as simple as the following example of a generic project spanning a twelve-week period.

Week #	Task/Milestone
1	Talk to potential customers; choose one
2	Develop project topic
3	Conduct background research
4	Gather equipment and project resources
5	Complete design iteration 1
6	Complete design iteration 2

7	Get feedback from customer(s)/modify
8	Perform analysis
9	Perform analysis
10	Preliminary design to customer
11	Final design to customer
12	Document results and write report

Once you've set this framework for your project, you can get an idea of how feasible your schedule is by detailing each week's activities; remember to budget time for the unexpected events that you have no control over, such as equipment breakdowns. You may find that it is nearly impossible to complete your task in the allotted time period. If that's the case, then make sufficient modifications to your schedule or project (or both) to overcome these shortcomings.

As you go out into the workforce, you'll find that project planning will contribute to a project's success. It absorbs a lot of time in the real world too, so you might as well get used to it!

Unofficial Senior Projects

Not all project work is done in a senior project course. Other opportunities are available to you in engineering societies, which facilitate the exchange of technical information by sponsoring design competitions or research activities that advance technical knowledge. Sometimes the projects are geared toward the specific technical needs of industry or society in general.

For example, the student chapter of the American Society of Mechanical Engineers (ASME) sponsors design competitions for innovative solar-powered vehicles, special wheelchair equipment, and all-terrain vehicles. In each instance, design objectives and requirements are given to a team of people who develop the most efficient, practical, and economical device that they can. In the case of a solar-powered vehicle, perhaps vehicle battery life is important. In the case of a special wheelchair project, perhaps a unique control algorithm is desirable.

The student chapter of the American Society of Civil Engineers (ASCE) sponsors yearly design competitions that you might want to participate in. The most notable are the bridge and concrete canoe design competitions. The bridge design competition encompasses many elements of an engineering project—design, analysis, optimization, and construction. For example, all bridges must be built within certain weight and size limitations. The only allowable construction materials are Popsicle sticks and glue. The structure is then loaded with weights until failure, and awards are given for the lightest bridge that carries the heaviest load.

The concrete canoe competition is a popular event among civil engineers. Again, certain size and weight constraints are imposed. However, all of the elements of an engineering project are involved, including cost. The civil engineering students must find funding to purchase the materials required for a four-man canoe. This includes cement, rebar, and other lightweight materials. After the research, design, and analysis are complete, the engineers construct the canoe by building a form, bending and welding rebar, and applying lightweight concrete. The most efficient design is judged by a series of canoe races. Usually, the lightest canoe wins!

Student Engineering Societies

You should not only participate in the student chapter of your engineering specialty (e.g., ASME, ASCE, IEEE, AIAA); you should also consider other engineering organizations, such as the Engineers Council, Society of Women Engineers, Tau Beta Pi, and Pi Tau Sigma. While the student chapters of the engineering specialties are important for contacts and other technical exchange of information, other student engineering organizations set policy, encourage engineering excellence, and educate future engineering students. (See page 133.)

The Politics

Many schools have Engineers Councils that are comprised of students from all sorts of engineering disciplines. This council serves to foster communication among the engineering disciplines. It also represents all engineering students to the governing body of the institution. The council establishes policies (proper student behavior, student/professor conflict resolution procedures, etc.) for all engineering students.

The council may encourage communication among engineering students by hosting an engineering career fair where representatives from engineering industries convene to share their company specialties with students. This process makes the student aware that the real-world engineering jobs and opportunities often involve many engineering disciplines. It's rare that any single engineering specialty would not have interactions with another discipline in order to complete a project. Remember, each engineer contributes his expertise to a large project that might involve many disciplines.

The council might stimulate alumni/student interactions by sponsoring an alumni breakfast and seminar. The purpose of this event is to show the student that the practicing engineer has succeeded and done well. It also encourages one-on-one interactions with the experienced alumni in different engineering fields. A broad understanding of the real engineering field is always useful.

The council also serves as the communication agency to the rest of the university, including the student body and the board of regents (or another governing entity). It functions primarily as an advocate for the engineering college, promoting engineering student ideas and issues of concern to the rest of the university. It also serves as a disciplinary review board which deals with student problems (e.g., health-related issues that cause bad grades or unethical student conduct such as cheating on an exam).

Another important function of the council is to encourage high school students to pursue an engineering career. One example is an "Adopt an Engineer" program, which allows high school students to match one-on-one with junior- and senior-level engineering students. The younger student is allowed to attend labs and lectures with the upperclassman. If one-on-one matching is not possible, the council arranges for the upperclassmen to teach basic engineering concepts to the high school student in a participative lab experiment. Young engineering students (as you should know by now) are enthusiastic about the hands-on engineering experience.

If your engineering school does not have an active Engineers Council or has never had one, consider starting one! Your leadership role in this effort not only will be self-fulfilling but will also look good on your résumé. Engineering employers value leadership abilities—so seize the opportunity if it's available!

The Brains

If you have good grades, consider joining an engineering honor society. The purpose of such organizations is to encourage engineering excellence among peers as well as others who might need help. Although some engineering disciplines have their own honor society (e.g., Pi Tau Sigma for mechanical engineers), the most notable nondiscipline-specific engineering honor society is Tau Beta Pi.

Once you've met Tau Beta Pi requirements, you're in it for life. They sponsor advanced engineering research activities that encourage and promote engineering excellence, and scholarships are granted for members who wish to pursue advanced degrees in specialty fields. Tau Beta

Pi also provides tutoring services. In this way, the organization passes along its brainpower to students who can take advantage of it.

Social Issues

It is important to recognize your unique individual characteristics. Remember that being an engineer is only a portion of your life. The engineering profession supports engineering societies and clubs that promote cross-cultural exchanges and work on gender-specific issues. Your school may have a minority engineering society or a Society of Women Engineers (SWE) that you could join.

"My experience in the Society of Women Engineers," says Ingrid Eng, "provided me with insight to deal with male workers in the field. This was useful since most construction-site workers are only used to dealing with male engineers." SWE also enables women to network with other women in the predominantly male profession. It sponsors nationwide conferences to promote a sense of belonging, and it provides a forum for meeting other women in the engineering profession. It also reaches out to women who are interested in engineering but need encouragement from others who have been through the process.

▪ 9 ▪

I AM AN ENGINEER ... NOW WHAT?

It's time to move into the real world. Time to make a living; time to contribute to your new profession; time to contribute to society as an engineer. No doubt you're excited about having more spare time, getting out of debt, and leading a normal life. However, there are some real-world issues to deal with now that don't get taught in school.

Finding your first job can be tricky. Although it's important to be technically competent in any engineering job, there are marketing aspects in landing your first job that you must be aware of.

Most engineering employers screen applicants for technical competence by looking at GPAs. If you're graduating from an established engineering school that has a rigorous curriculum, the employer already knows that you're competent. And so the key to getting your foot in the door and landing a great job is to sell your unique capabilities and qualifications. You must market yourself to the employer because there's going to be a lot of competition for these jobs from your fellow students, who are also competent engineers. Get the edge on the jobs available to your particular skills by following a few helpful hints, both from engineers who have been through the interviewing process and from those who have interviewed candidates.

Start Early

Consider thinking seriously about your first engineering job at least two semesters before you graduate. Many of the engineering employers start interviewing in the fall for spring graduates. So if you're planning to take advantage of early interviews, you must be prepared before they start in the fall of your senior year.

The Résumé

The first step is to write your résumé. Although you probably have a sense of how to write a generic résumé, let's get specific about an *engineering* résumé—format, appearance, emphasis, and style.

Format

The résumé should contain these major headings: name; permanent and school addresses; education with degree, major, and overall GPA; experience to include appropriate engineering part-time work and other school-related research projects; summary of major reports and publications; and professional affiliations. Do not exceed one page for your résumé. You may avoid a length problem by selecting a smaller, yet readable font for your résumé.

It is appropriate, however, to attach pages with information concerning technical reports, publications, and briefings. You may not have had these experiences yet unless you've had a very good summer job or a graduate student or professor who included you in their research. Hold the list of references sheet until the prospective employer asks for it.

Appearance

The résumé should be clean and neat. Engineers are usually well organized and meticulous. Avoid flashy fonts or other cutesy markings on the page.

Emphasis

Always emphasize the positive and the most important technical issues you wish to sell. If you're particularly proud of a technical paper that you co-authored with your major professor, give a brief synopsis of that rather than tell about a particular summer job you had as an office gofer. If you spearheaded a successful project for your engineering society, emphasize that rather than the job you had as a blueprint runner. Experience does not always mean a paying job.

Style

Engineers are concise in their writing habits. So get to the point! Be as short and terse as possible in writing your résumé. Don't spend time on flowery language, because nobody has time to read it. Engineers are very leery of pretty or slick-looking résumés, believing they may lack technical merit or content.

Where to Start

A sample résumé is shown below. It exemplifies many of the points that you should keep in mind as you develop your own résumé. Once you've composed your draft résumé, run it by professors, fellow students, and experienced engineers. Ask them for an honest assessment, and modify your résumé accordingly. Remember, the résumé will be introducing you to your prospective employer. Take it seriously!

JANE Q. ENGINEER

Campus Address	*Permanent Address*
1234 Street Place	5678 Lane Avenue
Anytown, State 55555-5555	Anytown, State 55555-5555
(Area Code) Work Phone	(Area Code) Home Phone
(Area Code) Home Phone	

JOB OBJECTIVE (One line, maybe two)
   Structural analyst for a major design firm with an emphasis on finite element solution techniques.

EDUCATION (Start with engineering; list others as appropriate)
   B.S. in Your Engineering Specialty (Expected Graduation Date in Day, Year)
   School, City, State. GPA: 3.8/4.0 (Major) 3.6/4.0 (Overall) (List both GPAs if major is higher)
   Emphasis on Control Theory

EXPERIENCE (List only three or four of the most relevant; don't worry about chronological order)
   Your University, City, State
   • Date—Position/Title
   Major accomplishments; primary activities or duties. (Emphasize technical work performed—one or two lines)

   A Significant Summer Technical Job, City, State
   • Date—Position/Title
   Major accomplishments; primary activities or duties. (Again, emphasize technical work, even if it's not related to your specialty. The scientific method is important in engineering!)

Independent Research Project Title, City, State
- Date—Engineering Student

This could be a significant senior project; a project for your engineering society; a special research activity for your professor. (Always emphasize your accomplishments *and* your contributions!)

Honors, Professional Affiliations, and Publications (You may not have an entry in all of these categories)

Honors. Recipient of the XYZ Scholarship; award for best project at AIAA competition; member of the Tau Beta Pi Engineering Honor Society

Affiliations. Member (or officer) of your professional society; member of the Engineers Council

Publications (Don't forget conference papers that your professor submits!). Authors, "Title," *Where Published*, Date

Source of Job Leads . . . Research

You would be wise to seek and consider as many opportunites as possible. No matter whether you're at the top or the bottom of your graduating class, be aggressive in your job search! It's rare that a "golden opportunity" will be laid at your feet.

First, make a list of all possible sources of job leads. That list might include the following major headings.

- *Summer/Part-Time Work Contacts.* Don't hesitate to call on former co-workers and bosses who might have a direct connection to job availability.
- *Professors.* Remember, you should know one or two fairly well by now. Professors have a lot of interaction with private industry and government.
- *Scholarship Sponsoring Agency.* The luncheon that you had with your sponsoring agency might provide an easy introduction.
- *Placement Office.* This might be a long shot but be sure to put your résumé on file here. Cover your bases!
- *Fellow Students/Friends/Family.* Network. Talk to people. Find out about opportunities from your Uncle Richard's cousin or Aunt Kathy's father-in-law. This might be a way to get ahead of other recent graduates who are seeking engineering employment too.

- *Professional Society Affiliations.* Don't forget about the contacts you've made as a result of your involvement in AIAA, ASCE, ASME, Engineers Council, etc. Maybe you had a guest speaker at one of your monthly meetings who wouldn't mind a phone call from you.
- *Newspaper.* The technical jobs listed in the classified ad section usually require some prior engineering experience, and would expect you to "hit the pavement running." Engineers fresh out of college don't always fit the bill, but call and find out about opportunities anyway to get an idea of the job market in your geographical location of interest.
- *Library.* This resource should be used to gather names, addresses, and phone numbers of potential contacts. Government publications, private organizations, and technical magazines list potential engineering employers in every region of the United States. Do a bit of research to get an idea of the types of engineering firms and corporations that exist in the United States.

Experiences of Those Who Have Been There

The resources that you use to find your first engineering job could provide the opportunity of a lifetime. If you don't pursue these job leads, you may not have many opportunities. Consider the experiences of seasoned engineers who have been in your shoes recently; they remember quite well how they got their first engineering job. The key to their success seemed to be networking and previous contacts. Few were just plain lucky—they all had to actively seek their own jobs and market their talents.

Gregg Skow graduated in December rather than May. Because there were fewer opportunities in December, he tried to use as many resources as possible in marketing himself. "I put my résumé in the placement office at school, but my success in getting my first engineering job was due to my friends and former colleagues at GTE." He had worked as a summer intern for GTE just before he graduated in December. "Fortunately, I maintained contacts within the company who knew about my capabilities, and I was ultimately offered a job over the telephone."

"I put my name and résumé in the placement center," said John Patterson, "and called on contacts from my summer work experiences, contacted my scholarship sponsor, and did library research. However, getting my first job resulted from the contacts that I developed during my part-time research job at school." When the Arizona Department of Transportation (ADOT) came to the University of Arizona to find potential engineers, they asked one of John's major professors, Dr. Jimenez, for recommendations. "As a result of my work experience and accomplishments with Professor Jimenez, he recommended me for an interview with ADOT."

Doug Gapp had a volunteer job with the city, working in the engineering inspections department. "I learned of the job through the placement office, but ultimately I got my first engineering job as a result of contacts and opportunities that grew out of this volunteer job." Doug's volunteer efforts eventually turned into a part-time paying job. "When Southwest Gas called the placement office looking for engineers, I fit the bill because of my city experiences with franchises."

Keep your options open and cover all bases, because you never know when that potential employer might call, looking for your unique talents.

Select and Make Contact

You've put your résumé in the placement office, researched firms at the library, talked to every potential lead that came to mind. Now it's time to make a few decisions.

Compared with people in many other professions, engineers are paid well—but don't base your job decisions on potential salary alone. When you grapple with the question of which engineering industry or firm to consider seriously, take a few factors into account. First, is there a particular type of engineering work that interests you more than others? For example, don't work for a testing laboratory if your first love is theoretical analysis. Second, is there a specific location that meets your lifestyle requirements? Don't live in the heart of Los Angeles if "getting away from it all" is important to you. Third, if at all possible, don't consider an industry or firm that is in economic trouble. (Get current information from your professors or other firms in your field of interest.) For example, if you're a mining engineer specializing in copper extraction and the copper industry is down, you may want to consider alternatives. The last thing you want to do is work for a company two years and get laid off. These short experiences may not give you enough time to develop your engineering skills and capabilities.

Keeping the above criteria in mind, select five to ten companies for serious consideration. Write down each company name, address, phone number, and contact person here.

| Company Name | Address | Phone # | Contact Person |

1.

2.

3.

4.

5.

6.

7.

8.

9.

10.

Boot Up Your Personal Computer

After you've completed your list of companies, take some action—it'll pay off. Dennis Roach received a lot of responses from the aerospace industry by contacting people. "I had several interviews and plant tours as a result of the effort I put into writing cover letters and sending out résumés."

Here's how to get started. First, use the information that you gathered in your research about each company to generate cover letters for your résumé. Remember that each cover letter should be specific to the technical needs of the potential engineering job. For example, if you've seen an advertisement in a technical journal or publication for new hires, state in a few paragraphs how you might fit in with the company and how you meet or exceed the job requirements as you know them. Follow the example cover letter below. (A few comments about content are given in italics.)

Date

Mr. John Q. Person
The Engineering Firm
1234 Anystreet
City, State XXXXX-XXXX

Dear Mr. Person,

(Paragraph 1. State why you're sending this information.)
I am responding to your recent advertisement in the *Technical Journal* for the entry-level engineering position. Currently, I'm finishing my last semester of nuclear engineering at the University of Anywhere and I am interested in opportunities at your firm.

(Paragraph 2. State how your interests and/or experiences meet the job requirements.)
Your work in nuclear waste management intrigues me. My major interest in school was studying the long-term effects of nuclear waste seepage into groundwater, and I've conducted research for Professor John Smith over the last year. We've recently published a paper in the *Journal of Nuclear Engineers* concerning our work. I am looking forward to discussing your requirements and my experience in an interview. *(Always mention that you're interested in a personal interview.)*

Sincerely,

Jane Q. Engineer

Attachment *(Attach your one-page résumé to this cover letter.)*

Make a Phone Call!

A few days after you've sent out your cover letter and résumé, follow up with a phone call. Don't bother or annoy the potential employer, but try to determine if they received your résumé and if everything is in order. You may want to buy a phone answering machine, because employers don't have time to play "telephone tag."

Set Up the Interview

If after another week you haven't received notification of a pending interview or a rejection letter, call the potential employer again. During this conversation, your goal is to schedule a personal interview. You may discover, however, that your résumé has slipped through the cracks, and now is a good time to fix whatever problems need to be fixed. Be aggressive without being pushy.

Interviewing

Here's the moment you've been waiting for—the moment when you market your capabilities and talents. Remember, the interview will determine whether or not the company is interested in you and whether or not you're interested in the company.

Follow these tips from experienced engineers who have been on both sides of the interviewing fence.

Go Prepared

The worst thing you can do is to go into an interview cold. John Patterson says that his research prior to the interview at the placement office made him feel more comfortable during the interview. It was like studying before a final exam—he just felt prepared. Do some detailed fact finding on the company. Read about their major products; their major customers; their financial history; their employment trends (size, mix, outlook). You don't have to memorize these facts, but having knowledge of them might be useful.

Next, look closely at the job requirements stated in the source of your information (e.g., job bulletin listing at the placement office or advertisement in a technical journal). Select key job requirement phrases, and write out how you meet or exceed each point. This will match your capabilities to the job requirements. You might even take this information with you to the interview, because there may be requirements that the interviewer should clarify.

Give Something

This is really important to a successful interview, because all employers like to see results-oriented people—those who can take a concept or idea and make reality from it. Take a sample report or publication; show senior project documentation (photographs); take a widget that you've designed; show documentation of a process or computer code that you developed. Offering a project to the interviewer will break the ice and give you a chance to speak comfortably about a topic that you're very familiar with.

Have a Can-Do Attitude

Always accentuate the positive in responding to the interviewer's questions. When you deal with your weaknesses (and we all have a few) explain how you've learned from your experiences—don't make up excuses. You may have all the engineering qualifications in the world, but if you're perceived as having a bad attitude, or are seen as arrogant or negative, you may not get the job. These qualities are the kiss of death in an interview. You must be capable of interacting with all types of people. The capable engineer with people skills will get the job over another capable engineer with no people skills.

Doug Gapp said that when he interviewed with the Southwest Gas Company, he hit it off really well with the vice president of engineering. "He made me feel very comfortable in the interview by encouraging me to clarify any points that I didn't understand during our discussion." Doug also remembers that the questions during the interview were not technical in nature; rather they were about goal setting (where do you want to be in five years?) and previous work experiences (how did you handle multiple job tasks?). The employer is more interested in your engineering potential than in your engineering experience at this stage of the game.

Ask Questions

Come prepared to ask an insightful question or two of the interviewer—details of job requirements; concerns about corporate status; direction of the company. How do you fit into their vision of where the company is headed? The interview is as much a review of your capabilities as it is a review of their company. The match must be there!

Follow Up

Don't be afraid to ask for follow-up information, such as the time frame in which an employer will make further decisions. Ask when you'll be notified about the outcome of your interview (e.g., rejection, plant tour, second interviews). You want to get an answer so you can plan for the future. On the other hand, if you know that this job isn't for you, don't hesitate to call your interviewer later to withdraw your name. If you expect the company to follow up with you, then you should follow up with them if you're not serious about the job.

If you've had a bad experience in the interview, such as a personality conflict with the interviewer, the company or the job may not have been properly represented. See if you can't get a better feeling for the company by establishing another contact person. Call the manager of the personnel department and voice your concern. Be frank and ask for another chance. Don't close your opportunities on the basis of one experience. You may be missing the opportunity of a lifetime.

Plant Tour

A plant tour is an invitation by a company to visit their operations. The purpose is to get a more in-depth feel for the company while other company representatives get to evaluate you. Travel and living expenses may or may not be paid by the company. For example, although I had a job offer from Boeing in Seattle, I would not accept the job without a plant tour. At that time, Boeing would not spring for the cost of an airplane ticket. I worked a deal with the personnel representatives—if I made my way to Seattle, they would pay for my living expenses (lodging and food). So I went on my plant tour.

Plant tours are very important in making a final decision. It's most often the first chance to speak with engineers rather than personnel representatives. You'll probably spend a full day meeting potential bosses and colleagues. It's your chance to ask candid questions of your prospective employer. Keep the following questions in the back of your mind as you discuss opportunities.

1. *What's the job really about?*
   Find out the nature of the work—is it primarily design- or analysis-oriented? Hopefully, you'll be interacting with a few engineers who are recently out of school. Be blunt in these informal discussions. Would you work with small component designs or large system designs? Would you have the appropriate support from other departments to successfully complete a task? What engineering software does the company use? Has the engineer described the nature of his or her current tasks?
2. *How is the working environment?*
   Come prepared to listen carefully and observe the working conditions. (Don't spend lots of time taking notes, unless it's to jot

down a name and telephone number.) See if you can pick up some of these gut reactions.

Do employees seem on edge?

Do they feel free to express their concepts or ideas to their managers?

Is there a sense of teamwork?

3. *How is life in the local community?*

   Ask questions about living conditions in the community. Don't hesitate to ask questions about your spouse's or children's concerns; your housing requirements; and your special interests or hobbies. Remember, there's life after 5 p.m., and you may not want to compromise your special concerns or needs for a job.

4. *Other issues*

   There are other factors that must be plugged into the job-hunting equation—not the least of which are salary and benefits. Money is a fact of life, and you must know that you'll be sufficiently compensated for your talents. At the end of your plant tour, if you haven't already, you should ask your host about the following issues:

- Range of starting salary—minimum and maximum
- Health benefits—medical, dental, eye, life insurance
- Vacation policy—two weeks, three weeks starting?
- Investment opportunities in the corporation—stock options in the company; 401K plans; matching employee contributions

After you've completed the plant tour process, write down your impressions. You may want to do this while the information is fresh in your mind. Use the above four questions to organize your thoughts and write them below.

Impressions of a Plant Tour

1. *What's the job really about?*

2. *How is the working environment?*

3. *How is life in the local community?*

4. *Other issues*

Making the Decision

Things should start to come together for you now. You're either near graduation or just beyond graduation. You've been exposed to the engineering job market, and hopefully you've had four or five interviews by now—maybe two or three plant tours. It's time to select your first technical job.

Regardless of whether or not you have your mind set on a particular job already, review your plant tour information. Start by comparing your responses to the four major questions. Which response is most important to you? Are the specific job requirements more important at this early stage in your career, or are the job benefits (other issues) more important?

John Patterson toured the plant of a major corporation in Salt Lake City. "This firm offered me a very high starting salary compared with other job offers I had. During the plant tour, however, an engineer made a comment that bothered me. He said that the firm hadn't given raises in two years. For that reason alone, I suspected that the company was having troubles, although the high-paying job sounded great to a struggling student." Fortunately, John didn't accept the job, and as he suspected, the company went out of business a few years later.

It's important to start your career with a company that is stable and has experienced engineers who can serve as mentors. You're at the learning stage in your engineering career, and you don't want to work for a company in crisis—they won't have time to mentor you. If you've written lots of positive comments about a particular firm, but your gut feeling is that something is wrong—something probably is. Follow up on your instincts, even if it means making a few phone calls. Ask your contacts quite frankly about your concern, and hopefully he or she will be kind enough to deal with you honestly.

Plant tours usually result in job offers, unless something really goes-wrong (if, for example, funding for your position gets cut). So be prepared to decide among the companies that gave you plant tours. There should be one clear match for you—maybe even two if you're lucky. After you receive formal notification, accept as soon as you are sure that the job is for you.

If you went through the job-search process and you came up with no job matches, read the next chapter—there's yet another option for you! Don't feel bad; some engineers have been through the job-hunting process only to discover that the timing or the situation wasn't right. View this as another opportunity!

· 10 ·

CONSIDER AN ADVANCED DEGREE... AND OTHER OPTIONS

When I graduated with my bachelor's degree, I was really burned out on school. I was tired of constant studying, working part-time, and having no money or spare time. I didn't have a life! What happened to the good old days when I went hiking, played sports, and read novels just for fun? My social life was practically nonexistent except for interactions with my study partners. For me, life was out of balance.

As a result, I was the last person to consider graduate school immediately after I received my bachelor's degree. I thought the graduate school curriculum would be impossibly hard, and because failure was not a part of my vocabulary, I felt that it was time to get out into the real world. Design a bridge; analyze a multistory structure; participate in a large building project—earn some money! I had five job offers to consider—a few that weren't too bad. But instead, I went to graduate school!

One of my job offers was unbelievable. An employer wanted to send me (all expenses paid) to the graduate school of my choice. My only obligation was to complete my master's degree in one calendar year. I didn't have a formal obligation to return to the company after graduation! That employer, of course, was Sandia National Laboratories.

I attended Purdue University, and I had a good experience. Many of the engineering concepts that I didn't completely understand or that I didn't get to explore in depth in undergraduate school became very clear to me in graduate school. I successfully completed my master's degree in the allotted time period and went to work at Sandia National Laboratories.

To Go or Not to Go . . . This Is the Real Question

Although you may have a job lined up, and your grades are good or even just average, you should consider graduate school. Don't consider money just yet, unless it involves family members. Explore your graduate school options by checking the appropriate boxes in Table 10-1. If the box or issue doesn't apply, mark NA for not applicable.

After completing the table, scan the number of boxes you've checked in each column, and compare them. Perhaps one particular issue is more important than another, and you may want to consider it more seriously.

The "Quest for Knowledge" Reason

Ideally, each engineer who decides to attend graduate school should base his or her decision on sound judgment—like Steve Doerr, Dave Kozlowski, and Keri Sobolik. "After working as an engineering intern

Table 10-1. Major Issues

Issues	Go to graduate school now	Don't go to graduate school now
Good Job Lined Up		
No Job Lined Up		
B Average or Greater in School		
Less Than B Average in School		
Spouse's Issues		
Children's Issues		
Parents' Issues		
Location Issues		
Other Personal Issues		

in the aerospace industry," said Steve, "I discovered that I had a thirst for knowledge concerning wind tunnel model testing. As a result, I went to graduate school to understand more details in that area of expertise." " I was always theoretically driven," said Dave, "and I just knew that a master's degree was for me." Keri mentioned that she wanted to work in the research end of engineering and that it required at least a master's degree to do so. "I learned through my thesis study that the research world of engineering was for me."

The Practical Reason

The reality of the world influences many of our decisions. "When I graduated in mechanical engineering in 1982, the country was in the middle of a recession," says Steve Sobolik. "Most of the opportunities at that time were for petroleum engineers in Texas. The aerospace industry wasn't hiring." Because job opportunities were limited, Steve considered graduate school more seriously. "When I went through the job-search process during my senior year, I simultaneously applied to graduate schools, just to cover all bases. As a result, I landed a research assistantship at Texas A&M." It turned out to be a valuable experience because he worked on a long-term project that gave him a better understanding of the engineering world.

Although Dennis Roach had good job offers from several major aerospace firms, he felt it was worth putting in a few more years of school for the future payoff. "After I researched my job opportunities in the aerospace industry, I realized that I was limiting myself to one industry. I had an interest in experimental mechanics from my CO-OP experiences, and I knew that this field of study would open more job opportunities for me. So I went to graduate school to study more of the experimental mechanics world."

Jon Rogers was interested in graduate school because his undergraduate professors had suggested he get a master's degree. "With their encouragement, I entered graduate school immediately after I received my bachelor's degree, and I was given a one-year research project complete with funding. After I completed my project, I taught undergraduate courses—something that I really enjoyed."

Reasons Not to Go . . . Now

Engineers decide not to attend graduate school for various reasons. The most common, however, is job opportunity. As Gregg Skow said, "Graduating in the fall semester when most recruiters come around in the spring was not the most ideal situation. Although I was very concerned about getting a job right out of engineering school, my backup plan was to attend graduate school. However, as luck had it, I got a job and never attended graduate school."

Although Doug Gapp was offered a fellowship for further studies in civil engineering, he turned it down. "I had an opportunity to work with a soils professor for an advanced degree, but my desire to work in the real world was too great at the time. I accepted a job with Southwest Gas right out of school, and it was the right decision for me," Doug said.

Tommy Goolsby's motto could be: If at first you don't succeed, try again! "For personal reasons, I went to work as a mechanical engineer for the booming oil industry, but I didn't get a chance at getting a master's degree because the company didn't encourage it. So I quit and did it on my own." He went back to UTEP to study his first love—mechanical design and experimental testing.

How to Apply

Here are some tips to consider when you apply to graduate school.

1. *Target a few schools.* Talk to your major professors, and select a few graduate programs; shoot for the moon!
2. *Write and ask for an assistantship.* If the opportunity doesn't come to you the way it did for Jon Rogers, go find it! Keri Sobolik wrote to several major engineering schools, and as a result, one offered her a research assistant position. Don't be shy. The worst thing that can happen is that you might receive a rejection letter, or a letter of acceptance and a request for $10,000 a year to attend. (You can always write back and say no!)
3. *Complete the application process.* Return the necessary paperwork with your letters of recommendation and transcripts. This shouldn't be very complicated.
4. *Take the Graduate Record Examination (GRE).* The GRE is required prior to entering graduate school; try to take it as early as you can. The test is divided into math and verbal skills. Send the scores to the graduate programs that you're considering.
5. *Consider other options.* Who said there is no such thing as a free lunch? Many corporations sponsor advanced degree programs for their employees. Dave Kozlowski said, "I had a chance to work for a firm that encouraged part-time graduate studies at Colorado State University, but I chose a company that paid for me to attend

graduate school full-time." Perhaps, before you accept any job offer, you may want to ask your employer about such opportunities.

Thinking about a Ph.D.?

Although it might be a bit premature, you may want to set a goal now to get a Ph.D. in engineering. In speaking with my colleagues who have Ph.D.s, a few points can be noted about the degree. The first is that it commands a certain amount of respect. With a Ph.D., the world views you as an expert in a highly specialized field of study. "It can mean that you serve as a principal investigator on large projects," says Dr. Steve Doerr. Such responsibilities can be very professionally gratifying. Dr. Jon Rogers adds that the degree allows you to stay in academia to teach, research, and consult. "Since the degree means that you're very highly specialized in one area, it limits your job opportunities." You may become overqualified for some engineering positions. Ph.D.s most often work in research labs and universities. This can definitely be very intellectually satisfying.

The Professional Engineer (PE)

Another option is to go the professional engineering route. The PE is a licensed engineer who is expert in his field of study. State laws require that certain types of drawings and plans, for example, must have a PE stamp on them—especially those engineering projects involving the general public. This method of control assures society that a competent professional has reviewed the information for correctness and that the engineer takes responsibility for those plans or drawings.

John Patterson is a PE, and he found it necessary for his future job advancement. "After I worked a few years as a civil engineer, it was clear that my job opportunities were greater with the PE stamp." Most private consulting firms are owned or run by PEs. Many local, state, and federal engineering agencies are also heavily staffed with PEs.

So how do you get a PE stamp? The rules vary from state to state, but generally the engineer is required to pass two different examinations and have some engineering experience. The first requirement is to pass a Fundamentals of Engineering (EIT) exam. It's typically an eight-hour exam that requires lots of knowledge from your sophomore- and junior-level coursework—basic dynamics, mechanics, fluids, etc. Once you've passed that exam and worked a few years, then you're eligible to take the PE exam in your specialty field. If you're interested in this process, contact the local chapter of your engineering society or call the state engineer's office. Even if you're not sure that you'll ever require a PE stamp, take the EIT anyhow. The chances of passing the EIT will be much greater while this information is still fresh in your mind. After a few years in the business, you can then take the final PE exam if you want to.

Just Do It!

As you reflect on your career options, I hope that you have a better understanding of the engineering profession—one that will help you make the right decision. Since this might be a lifetime career, you want to make sure that you're satisfied. When you head down the engineering path you should feel that you've made the right choice, but at times you may feel frustrated.

Remember that engineering is a broad field, and although you may enter the profession as a designer or research analyst, you may end up as a manager or a salesman. I've spent my entire professional career performing scientific work that I knew I wanted to do since I was five years old, and now, as an engineering manager, I'm responsible for the growth of *other* engineers and scientists. I'm a "people" person, and I have the opportunity to combine those skills with my scientific skills for an entirely new, nontechnical challenge. Don't ever think that you have to be strictly engineering-focused for the rest of your life.

You will have twists and turns in your professional path, but my final advice to you is don't shy away from them. Learn from them, grow as a person, and find opportunities from them.

Appendix

Associations and Organizations for the Engineering Student

Following is a list of engineering societies and institutes that might be helpful to you. Don't hesitate to write or contact any of these groups. They're there to assist you in any way they can.

If you need more comprehensive information on any of these groups (brief description, budget, staff, members, meetings, publications), it's available in the *Encyclopedia of Associations* at the reference desk in your local library.

Professional Engineering Organizations

American Institute of Aeronautics and Astronautics (AIAA)
The Aerospace Center
370 L'Enfant Promenade SW, 10th Floor
Washington, DC 20024
(202) 646-7400

Society for Mining, Metallurgy, and Exploration (SME)
PO Box 625002
Littleton, CO 80162-5002
(303) 973-9550

American Society of Mechanical Engineers (ASME)
345 E. 47th St.
New York, NY 10017
(212) 705-7722

American Institute of Chemical Engineers (AICHE)
345 E. 47th St.
New York, NY 10017
(212) 705-7338

Institute of Electrical and Electronics Engineers (IEEE)
345 E. 47th St.
New York, NY 10017
(212) 705-7900

American Society of Agricultural Engineers (ASAE)
2950 Niles Rd.
St. Joseph, MI 49085-9659
(616) 429-0300

American Society of Civil Engineers (ASCE)
345 E. 47th St.
New York, NY 10017
(212) 705-7496

Institute of Industrial Engineers (IIE)
25 Technology Park/Atlanta
Norcross, GA 30092
(404) 449-0460

Gender-Specific and Cultural Engineering Organizations

National Society of Black Engineers
1454 Duke St.
Alexandria, VA 22313-5588
(703) 549-2207

Society of Hispanic Professional Engineers
5400 E. Olympic Blvd., Suite 210
Los Angeles, CA 90022
(213) 725-3970

Society of Women Engineers (SWE)
345 E. 47th St., Room 305
New York, NY 10017
(212) 705-7855

Engineering Honor Societies

Alpha Pi Mu (Industrial)
PO Box 934
Blacksburg, VA 24063-0934
(703) 231-6656

Chi Epsilon (Civil)
B-15 Nedderman Hall
Univ. of Texas at Arlington
Arlington, TX 76014
(817) 469-8668

Eta Kappa Nu (Electrical)
Box HKN-UMR
Univ. of Missouri-Rolla
Rolla, MO 65401
(314) 341-6400

Omega Chi Epsilon (Chemical)
McNeese State Univ.
Dept. of Chemical Engineering
Box 91375
Lake Charles, LA 70609
(318) 475-5865

Pi Tau Sigma (Mechanical)
Tennessee Technological Univ.
Dept. of Mechanical Engineering
PO Box 5014
Cookeville, TN 38505
(615) 372-3254

Sigma Gamma Tau (Aerospace)
Syracuse University
Dept. of Mechanical and Aerospace Engineering
151 Link Hall
Syracuse, NY 13244-1240
(315) 443-4366

Tau Beta Pi Association
PO Box 8840, University Sta.
Knoxville, TN 37996-0002
(615) 546-4578